REVISED AND EXPANDED EDITION

BROTHERS, LUST, & LOVE

Thoughts on Manhood, Sex, and Romance

REVISED AND EXPANDED EDITION

BROTHERS, LUST, & LOVE

Thoughts on Manhood, Sex, and Romance

WILLIAM JULY II

DOUBLEDAY

NEW YORK · LONDON · TORONTO · SYDNEY · AUCKLAND

PUBLISHED BY DOUBLEDAY

a division of Bantam Doubleday Dell Publishing Group, Inc.

1540 Broadway, New York, New York 10036

DOUBLEDAY and the portrayal of an anchor with a dolphin are trademarks of Doubleday, a division of Bantam Doubleday Dell Publishing Group, Inc.

Book design by Julie Duquet

Library of Congress Cataloging-in-Publication Data

July, William.

Brothers, lust, & love : revised and expanded thoughts on manhood, sex, and romance / by William July II. — 1st ed.

p.   cm.

1. Man-woman relationships—United States.   2. Afro-American men—Psychology.

3. Afro-American men—Sexual behavior.   I. Title.

HQ801.J85   1998

306.7—dc21   97-52284

CIP

ISBN 0-385-49149-2

May 1998

First Edition

1   3   5   7   9   10   8   6   4   2

CONTENTS

LOVE

*Dedicated to my mother for making me practical,
my father, for making me wise,
and my sister, for turning a brat into a gentleman*

Love is patient, love is kind. It does not envy, it does not boast, it is not proud. It is not rude, it is not self-seeking, it is not easily angered, it keeps no record of wrongs. Love does not delight in evil but rejoices with the truth. It always protects, always trusts, always hopes, always perseveres.

1 CORINTHIANS 13:4–7

ACKNOWLEDGMENTS

First and foremost, I give honor to God. Thank you for allowing me to be in your service as an instrument for this message.

One tough thing about acknowledging people is that you don't have enough room to thank everybody. I really need to start at birth and list everyone who has ever come into my life from that moment. It is the sum of all those energy exchanges, both good and bad, that make us who we are. Of course, I can't do that. But here's a highlight of those who helped to make this dream a reality.

My interest in the written word started when I was about three years old. When my mother, father, and sister didn't want me to know what they were saying, they'd spell it out loud right there in front of me. They'd laugh as they went through their coded conversations. Meanwhile, I was utterly frustrated. That alone made me want to learn to read more than anything else in the world. I credit them with sparking my interest in the written word.

I also want to thank several of my teachers for nurturing my skills and love for writing. My second-grade teacher, Mrs. Carter, who helped me discover a gift for writing. My fifth-grade teacher, Mrs. Hughes, who praised my writing and encouraged me to continue. My seventh-grade teacher, Mrs. Gutierrez, for seeing that my work was acknowledged with an award. My high school English teacher, the late Lady Catley, who pushed me to the tough A's when I wanted to settle for the easy C's. My professors at Texas Southern University, espe-

cially Dr. Nell Cline and Dr. Betty Thompson Taylor, for un-
leashing my fervor for the written word in their classes.

I offer a prayer of peace and love for all my friends. Special
people who honor me with a special place in their hearts. I also
want to thank those who have served as my think tank and idea
laboratory: Tracey Benford, Dobbin Bookman, Greg Carter,
Michelle Clayton, Pedro Gomez, Charles Robinson, Eric
Robinson, and Tony Weathersby.

Much gratitude to the authors and writers who unselfishly
took the time to help me along the way. Some of them offered
kind and sincere encouragement. Others gave me a huge help-
ing hand as I climbed up the ladder: Apollo, Anita Bunkley,
Khephra Burns, Dr. Larry Davis, Audrey Edwards, Dr. Julia
Hare, Dr. Nathan Hare, E. Lynn Harris, Dr. Earl Hutchinson,
Lisa Jones, Clarence Major, Dr. Rosie Milligan, Jess Mowry,
Ella Patterson, Rev. Dr. Sheron Patterson, Valerie Shaw,
Claudette Sims, Don Spears, Jewel Diamond Taylor, Susan Taylor, and Ginger Whitaker. Good things happen when you plant
a seed.

I am thankful to the magazines, newspapers, and journals
that have published my articles and columns over the years:
*Essence, Upscale, Black Elegance, Being Single, Today's Black Woman,
New Visions, Papyrus, Our Texas,* and many others.

Love and blessings go out to each of the thousands of individuals who purchased the self-published version of this book
last year and blasted it to the best-seller list. A special thanks to
the small black booksellers of this country for giving me shelf
space when nobody else would.

A loving hug and kiss to my wife, Jamie, whom I met when I
was still selling my first book from the trunk of my car. Thanks
for standing by me and being my personal angel. I also thank

you for living with my idiosyncratic personal rituals. It takes a writer to love a writer.

A big thanks to my agent, Denise Stinson, for taking care of business.

I've been saving a huge round of applause for last. To the Doubleday team for infusing their talent, excitement, and positive energy into this book. A huge thanks to the editor of my dreams, Janet Hill; working with her has been a blessing. Thanks to Jean Traina for a super cover design. An ongoing thanks to Patricia Blythe and the publicity and marketing people, without whom time would stand still. And I don't want to leave out all the people turning the wheels behind the scenes, from the mailroom to the printing press to the president. This has truly been a team effort. Peace, love, and wellness to you all.

I gratefully acknowledge the following publishers and authors for allowing me to quote them in this book:

"Dogcatcher Quiz" from *Himpressions: The Blackwoman's Guide to Pampering the Blackman,* by Valerie Shaw.
Copyright © 1993, 1996 by Valerie Shaw
Reprinted by permission of HarperCollins Publishers, Inc.

An excerpt from the book *Beyond O.J.,* by Dr. Earl Ofari Hutchinson, Ph.D.
Copyright © 1996 by Dr. Earl Ofari Hutchinson, Ph.D.
Reprinted by permission of Middle Passage Press

An excerpt from the book *A Return to Love,* by Marianne Williamson
Copyright © 1992 by Marianne Williamson
Reprinted by permission of HarperCollins Publishers, Inc.

An excerpt from the essay ''Ghettocentrism'' by Deborah
Mathis
Copyright © 1993 by Deborah Mathis
as it appeared in the book *Thinking Black,* Crown Publishers

An excerpt from the book *Entitled to Good Loving,* by Audrey B.
Chapman
Copyright © 1995 by Audrey B. Chapman
Reprinted by permission of Henry Holt & Company, Inc.

REVISED AND EXPANDED EDITION

BROTHERS, LUST, & LOVE

Thoughts on Manhood, Sex, and Romance

INTRODUCTION

Many people will look at the cover photo of this book and wonder what kind of person I am. Hopefully, most of these assumptions will be good. It's normal and natural to make initial assumptions about people based on appearances. But in so doing, we have to remind ourselves that physical appearances don't always tell us everything about a person. For example, the cover photo for this book is the well-orchestrated combination of design, lighting, makeup, and an Armani suit, all intended to convey a specific image of William July the author.

But as I wrote this introduction, I was wearing a pair of Levi's jeans, a T-shirt, and some Nikes; that's the way I'm dressed most often. When I'm pumping gas into my car, going to the bank, or making a midnight ice-cream run, I'm not William July the author; I'm a large black man in jeans, a T-shirt, and Nikes. To some people, that still isn't a big deal. But there are those who may be alarmed by the presence of a big black guy because their minds are filled with stereotypes. But what they don't know is that there's much, much more to me than the color of my skin.

However, that's a perfect example to illustrate the essence of this book. *Brothers, Lust, and Love* was written to show that black men are more than meets the eye. Like all of God's human creations, we're three-dimensional beings composed of mind, body, and spirit. *Brothers, Lust, and Love* is an affirmation of the three-dimensional nature of black men. By openly questioning the stereotypes surrounding black men, their feelings of lust and love, I pose critical questions about the way black men are viewed in America. This book asks those who are not black males to think and reason about us instead of simply falling back on preset beliefs and distorted ideas. It is a fresh and bold examination of the everyday realities surrounding black men in their lives and relationships.

This book is not the ravings of an angry black man. It's not a frivolous book either. Nor is it the lamenting of a buppie. It's a search for truth that defies stereotypes about black men and their relationships. In the search for truth, this book is daring enough to question the behaviors of black and nonblack, married and single, male and female, young and old, straight and gay. Some parts are humorous. Some are sobering. Some are sensual. But I warn the reader now: All of it won't be easy to digest. *Brothers, Lust, and Love* was not written to be politically correct rhetoric seeking an easy amen.

As you read *Brothers, Lust, and Love,* remember that my words come from the perspective of love and healing. I am attempting to recover a human image of black men that has been lost somewhere in myths and stereotypes. This is one man's attempt to grasp his humanity, a self-therapy aimed at understanding myself and the forces that have shaped me into who I am. My words are those of one man who is offering an examination of his own life, lust, and love as a window to present ideas, conversations, and issues that will help all men and women see themselves better in their relationships as friends, co-workers, lovers, married couples, and even strangers passing on the street.

This book is more accurate and timely than a thousand studies by so-called experts could ever be, for one simple reason: this time the experts aren't speaking for me, I'm speaking for myself. I'm the man they all claim to know so well. But the experts, with all their statistics and media images, never seem to tell my story right. The fact about black men is that nobody can know our world as we do. We are among the most misunderstood, misquoted, and misrepresented people on earth.

Brothers, Lust, and Love is one more small step toward setting the record straight about the realities of black men. What's beamed at America on television doesn't represent all, or even most, black men. The majority of us are hardworking, taxpaying, common Americans who get up and go to work every morning. Millions of ordinary heroes, black men who work hard, strive to improve themselves, and respect women. Men who have lives that defy stereotypes, negative statistics, and the destructive images so often found in the media. Therein is found the strength of this book. On these pages are real words from an ordinary black man. That's a refreshing change. A separation of the facts from the fiction.

But above all, in *Brothers, Lust, and Love* I wish to engender a coming together, not a pushing apart. The words herein are seeded with love and hope for all relationships. Many relationships of today are in shambles because we lack the compassion and understanding necessary to experience true love. Instead, many people are deluded by forms of conditional love that don't require them to make the sacrifices and achieve the growth necessary to really experience love. To experience true love, we all have to start with an examination of our own hearts.

My prayer is that reading *Brothers, Lust, and Love* not only will give people a new understanding of black men and their relationships but will help them examine their own hearts. That's because self-examination ultimately leads to the blossoming of self-love. From the blossom of self-love comes new seeds of love that we share with others. And that love is the only power that can transform our lives and personal relationships from ones of constant struggle to peace and fulfillment.

BROTHERS

Mr. Right

Six feet three inches of man chiseled from black marble. He weighs in at 215 lean pounds. The ripples in his stomach were custom-cut with a diamond drill. His deep voice rolls like the waves of the ocean. His biceps, triceps, and chest were carved by Michelangelo. Deep innocent eyes, full lips, and a hard regal nose compose the boyish smile on his face. A tight waist and long, strong legs round out his perfect figure.

He graduated *cum laude* from Howard, received his MBA/JD from Harvard. In Europe, he did a stint at the London School of Economics. Then he lived in Paris while studying at the Sorbonne. He's the star of a Wall Street investment banking team during the week. But on weekends he unwinds with his jazz quartet and flows a few notes from his sax at a cozy little club uptown. He's active in his church, community, and all the local charities. His lavish parties are a roll call of elite social-ites, politicians, and celebrities. But despite his busy schedule and fame, he still makes time to shoot hoops in the park every Saturday morning with the kids from his old neighborhood. They all admire him like a big brother.

After a hard day in the wilderness of high finance, he skips the after-hours drinking and unwinding rituals and hurries home to you. Mr. Right always leaves all of his work and wor-ries at the office. He would never come home with papers to read or a project to wrap up. Home time is for you, the cen-ter of his life. He draws your bubble bath and leaves your favorite wine chilling next to the tub. While you unwind in the candlelight and bubble bath, he serenades you with a tape of his jazz quartet doing a song he wrote for you. As you swoon in the luxury, he puts the final touches on a sumptuous dinner. It's a gourmet dish he learned to prepare while he was living in France. Something simple but elegant. After your bath, he massages your feet and rubs you with fragrant massage oil while attentively listening to you talk about your day. Then he serves you dinner on the penthouse patio facing the setting sun.

Later that night, you entwine in lovemaking. He holds you, cradling you against his big, firm chest. He begins with soft but masculine stroking of your skin. His patient hands travel to every place on your body. Deep vibrations from his heavy voice are music to your ears. You get cold chills down your spine as he kisses your body in slow, soft circles. His lovemaking is gentle and firm, hard and soft, fast and slow . . . His masculinity overcomes you when you grab his muscular arms and feel them throb with his every movement. His scent drives you wild. The rhythm of his hips is hypnotic. Instinctively, he finds and holds the right spot. Then he waits patiently for you. He has never been first, always waiting for the signal from your body telling him to meet you at the climax of passion.

He's the perfect man for you.

Wake up, you're dreaming. This all-in-one man doesn't exist!

Being a captain of finance is time-consuming and totally draining. If he were such a powerhouse investment banker, he'd always be working. When he was home, it would be to sleep, not to rub you down. Besides, he'd have another office at home where he'd spend the last of his waking hours in preparation for the next day just so he could keep up with the hectic pace at the office.

Affection would be reduced to benign hellos and good mornings as you passed each other in the bathroom. Sex would have to be planned and scheduled between other, more important activities. As for his weekends blowing tunes with Grover Washington, Jr., he wouldn't have the time. If he played the sax it would've been years ago in high school and by now he'd have forgotten how to even hold a saxophone, much less how to blow an even note. What about his wonderful body? Possible but not probable. This man would be so into his work that he'd either get fat as a hog from all the stress or have the string-bean body of Jack Sprat from not having time to eat right.

Cinderella is out there looking for Prince Charming: the perfect man with money, looks, and charisma, who wants to worship her. My friend Charlotte has always been that way. In her mid-thirties now, she's still trying to find Mr. Right.

While she was in college, Charlotte's idea of the perfect man was based totally on excitement. She dated only men with frat letters, a sports car, or what she called a "super-fine" body. She got all that in the shimmering black body of Dell. He was a hard bad-boy type from Los Angeles attending a nearby school on a basketball scholarship. Not exactly the man her parents had in mind when they sent her off to Spelman. Her parents would never have approved of Dell, and that made it even more exciting. She had another nice-guy type she took home to Momma. But Dell was the man who got her juices flowing. His body was tight and smooth. He had a rippled stomach, a tattoo on his chest, and a mean grimace etched on his charcoal face. His words were bad and his temper was short. He'd blow his horn when he pulled into the parking lot and unlock her door without moving from behind the wheel. He hardly even gave hello kisses. Then it was straight back to his room for some "thumpin' and bumpin'." Charlotte fell for his brusque ways. His primal persona was attractive to a little "black American princess" raised to marry a doctor or lawyer.

Charlotte remembers in laughter, "After a round in bed with him, I'd drop straight to sleep."

But the fun in bed ended when Charlotte found out she was pregnant. Dell bailed out the back door when he heard the news. He refused to see her and denied that the baby was his. He accused her of sleeping with other men, even his friends. To keep the secret from her parents, Charlotte was forced to borrow the money for an abortion from friends. Dell never spoke to her again. After a knee injury, he was forced to quit the team. Later, he headed back to LA. So much for her bad-boy fantasy.

After graduation, Charlotte began to look at her future and decided she wanted a more refined and stable man in her life. The kind who gave her visions of a home in the suburbs, kids, and Links meetings. She wanted a "good man" (i.e., the type she wouldn't give the time of day in college). She joined some professional organizations and became active in volunteering for charities and political campaigns—all the places she figured she could find a good man. One year, nine banquets, and four political campaigns later, she finally met a good man. He was Gerald, the ultimate eighties buppy—a young, thin, and stylish CPA. He was bulleting up the ladder at a Big 8 accounting firm, and Charlotte felt she was catching him at the right time. He even looked the part—Brooks Brothers blue suit, silk tie, crisp white shirt, and Polo glasses on a little almond face.

But Gerald didn't turn out to be the man of Charlotte's dreams. Instead he was the wimp of her nightmares. He was totally into his career and rarely made time for her. All of his socializing was centered on the company. His definition of getting loose on the weekend was drinking a Heineken straight from the bottle at the home of one of his obsessed fast-track co-workers while discussing the details of office politics. Making matters worse, he was a pushover. Unlike Dell, Gerald made it a point never to disagree with Charlotte. He always cowered down when she became angry. Their lackluster relationship was reflected in the bedroom too. She didn't have an animalistic lust for him, as she had for Dell. Sometimes she would rather be doing her nails than screwing Gerald. Sex with him was a chore. Once he finally finished neatly removing his clothes, he put on a quick and boring performance under the sheets. Most of the time, she couldn't tell whether he was coming or having a seizure. The good-man Mr. Right had to go.

Then Charlotte turned inward. She decided Mr. Right must be an aesthetically oriented man. A man of the arts, a musician, a poet, or an actor. Eventually she ran into Rafael, an intellectual. He worked as a waiter in a popular upscale restaurant. Rafael was a chic man with a blasé attitude toward everything except his acting career and his poetry. He had big full shoulders, a reddish clay-brick skin tone, and a hard masculine exterior that made her swoon. The only problem was that Rafael didn't like to work. In three months, he'd had three different jobs—quitting each because of manufactured reasons. "I'm too good for that job," or "My boss is an idiot," he'd storm. Charlotte tried to be supportive. But when he started borrowing money with empty promises to repay, it was time for him to go. Mr. Right works.

The search for the perfect man is unrealistic. The fictional Mr. Right has everything in one package. But no man is going to be perfect in every category on your checklist. Compromise is almost a certain eventuality. "Compromise" isn't a dirty word. But "settling" is. Settling for less than quality is a bad thing that will haunt you every day. But compromising and accepting that everything won't be like the pages of a romance novel is just realistic.

I'm not proposing that women simply settle for the first thing that comes along. What I am suggesting is that women seriously examine the meaning of a man in a relationship. Are you seeking a financial partner, a stud, a friend, or a soul mate? A financial partner is a business deal. A stud you can find anywhere, anytime. A friend doesn't need to be your husband or boyfriend, or to sleep with you. But a soul mate is all-encompassing. That is the man who complements your being.

> *SBF seeking Mr. Right. Must be 6′3″, 215, have a mustache, degree in law or medicine from Ivy League institution, good singer or poet, former pro athlete, bilingual (preferably French or Italian), income over six figures or demonstrate potential for such within next twenty-four months. Must never have been hurt in a previous relationship. Never married and no children a must.*

Okay, that's a bit of an overstatement. But I've read some personal ads that are ridiculously specific. That's how outlandish the requirements of some women are. It's no small wonder they so often end up in twisted relationships. If you design by physical appearance, you're playing the lottery. It will probably get you hurt and disappointed. It's as though you're trying to fit the proverbial square peg into a round hole. You can't design by physical appearance or superficial traits and expect a real person to be that way.

The majority of women are going to have to make some realistic adjustments in what they want. First of all, there are more black women in the United States than black men. Then subtract the brothers behind bars; those brothers who, like you, are seeking Mr. Right; and the married ones. The pool of available men shrinks. From the remaining percentage, only a fraction are college-educated. Even fewer boast prestigious professional occupations. And of the small group remaining, only a handful command incomes of six figures or more. Within that exclusive circle, generally only women with similar incomes and backgrounds or absolutely heart-stopping looks will be able to get those men. Last, let us not forget, those men know they're in demand, and most don't mind reminding you of that.

Depressing? Not necessarily. All that doesn't mean that there are no good men out there. It just points to the need for re-education. It's all about your perspective. What is it that you want from a man? If "good man" means money, you're on the wrong track. If "good man" means a ticket to personal happiness, you're drifting in the wrong direction. If you want money, get your own, it's better that way. If you need fulfillment, that's a solo project that should precede your next relationship. The majority of women are going to have to find and love a man who is not riding a white stallion. Instead he may be driving a white Hyundai. But what if he really loves you? Isn't that enough? Or is a prerequisite for love having an office with degrees framed on the wall, a sailboat, and a Porsche?

There are some eligible black men out there who are at the top. Men making big money, wielding power, and floating in prestige. But they're the exception, not the rule. Should you settle? No. But you should learn to look beyond the exterior to the man inside. Some Mr. Rights are the unsung heroes of our society. Ordinary men who just make a good decent living and try to pay their bills on time. Unfortunately, they are invisible men to many women.

Ladies, do you know what the fantasy Ms. Right is for most black men? It's to have a woman really love and accept us for

who we are. There are some reality checks needed. The Cinderella and Superman images are myths. Reality is who you go
to bed with every night. And if you're going to bed alone,
check yourself. Maybe you're the reason. Perhaps you're waiting for someone perfect to come and sweep you away to Fantasy Island. Are you perfect in every way? If not, do yourself a
favor and develop a realistic idea of who Mr. Right actually is.
There may be someone out there waiting for you now. But he
probably doesn't fly through the air wearing a cape.

THINGS TO THINK ABOUT

1. What are my criteria for choosing a man? Why?

2. Do I have Cinderella views on love and relationships?

3. Are the qualities I seek most in a man financial, physical, or spiritual assets?

4. Do I judge men by my own standards or those of friends, family, and co-workers?

5. Have I settled for the wrong man in the past? Why?

6. Have I evaluated myself and the kind of mate I would make?

7. Have I developed a realistic idea of who Mr. Right will be?

Hello, How Are You?

In silence, I rode seven floors alone on an elevator with a black woman.

We momentarily made eye contact as I entered the elevator. But in a quick and sharp move she focused her eyes on her watch. On the surface, what may have seemed to be a casual time check wasn't that at all. It was a well-practiced cold shun that, to be honest, hurt my feelings. However, I still managed to mumble a "Hello," which she completely ignored. That cold gesture was her greeting and goodbye, the extent of our communication. By avoiding eye contact and filling the elevator with her gruff vibes, the young woman made it clear that she didn't intend to say a word to me. But all of that was unnecessary. I wasn't interested in flirting, asking for her phone number, or diving into bed with her. I simply wanted to say hello.

Even though they happen every day, scenarios like this are difficult to digest. This type of encounter always leaves me with a cold and hollow feeling. The way I see it, we're in a sad state of affairs when people are so suspicious of one another that they can't even exchange a simple greeting. But it's usually that way when the paths of black men and women cross. There's an immediate wall of tension, and we too often pass each other in total silence. It's an all too familiar scene acted out daily in offices, schools, and countless casual intersections: grocery stores, shopping malls, libraries, gyms, etc.

Though it happens often, I don't think I'll ever be comfortable with it. It hurts when I attempt to initiate a friendly conversation, or simply say "Good morning," and my actions are summarily dismissed by a hard, blank stare. I respect and appreciate black women. They are strong and gifted creations. Their presence is such that they can't be ignored. Invisible they are not. When I speak to a black woman on the street, it's my way of acknowledging the great gift that she is. It's not unlike when I kick my head up to a brother on the street and say "Whassup?" It's on this human-to-human level that I approach women in our casual intersections.

I know some men who have adopted a code of silence to cope with women who don't speak. They simply don't speak unless they are spoken to first. This way, they're assured that their kindness will be reciprocated. In other words, they won't be picking their cracked faces up off the floor. I've experimented with the silent treatment, but that approach seems just as ludicrous as when women don't speak to men. Two wrongs don't make a right. What we need is more friendly communication, not icy stare-downs in silence.

Sometimes when my hello falls on cold ears, I feel like turning around and shouting, "Baby, I'm sorry he treated you that way but it wasn't my fault!" But, of course, there's no reason to embarrass her or to make a fool of myself. Then again, I've actually considered keeping a printed speech in my attaché case to explain that I was simply making a small friendly gesture. Then, when I spoke to a woman and received no reply, I could chase her down and hand her a copy. But that wouldn't work, because I would be dismissed as crazy (rightfully so).

Speaking honestly, I know there are brothers out there who howl like dogs and hiss like reptiles and seem to make a practice of invading a woman's personal space. They stand in front of buildings, on construction sites, and at the windows of aerobics studios staring, hissing, growling, panting, barking, and yelping. I don't blame women for not wanting to speak to those men because they're not being respectful. If those cat calls are their way of saying hello, one can only imagine what they'd say or do next.

It is true that some men will say "Hello" and their next words are the same old clichés from the Official Book of 1001 Weak Lines. However, there are lots of genuinely sincere men out there who may just want to strike up a friendly and harm- less conversation. I believe in respecting a woman and her space. On behalf of men like myself, my appeal to women is simple. Learn to distinguish the gentlemen from the German shepherds. Whether a man is a gentleman or German shepherd is evident in the way he speaks to a woman when she crosses his path. The speech of a German shepherd is clichéd lines, cat calls, and lewd vocabulary because the German shepherd has more on his mind than just a simple hello. But a gentleman always speaks to women in a respectful and dignified manner. When a gentleman says hello, he's only being friendly.

Likewise, I will make an appeal to all those men who don't approach women with courtesy and respect. Learn some man- ners. You make it hard for the good men of the world to even hold a friendly conversation with a woman. Don't hiss, bark, and "Say, baby" your way up to a woman. Just say, "Hello, how are you?" And if a woman doesn't respond, don't call her a name as she walks away. Maybe she has a lot on her mind. It's possible that she didn't hear you. Who knows? Just go on with your day knowing you did your part to pass some positive energy. If she was in fact trying to be malicious, her problem is something she'll have to deal with sooner or later. Don't make it your problem too.

Having said all that, it would be wrong of me to allow the reader to think I speak of all black women. I have received numerous hellos in return. Moreover, I have received unsolic- ited smiles, hellos, and good mornings. To those women, I thank you for bringing some light into my life. Those positive encounters have lasted in my mind as hope and inspiration, and have overcome the negatives. Indeed, there are many black women who are aware of this communication problem and actively do their part to reverse it.

But there are still many like the woman on the elevator. I haven't given up on her. I guess I'll just have to keep speaking until she says hello. If you're like the woman on the elevator, get real. It won't cost you one dollar to return a smile or say hello. In fact, you will find that you made not only someone else's day better but yours as well. Do your part to break the silence. Start smiling and pass the good spirits.

THINGS TO THINK ABOUT

1. When men say hello to you in a respectful manner, do you respond by saying hello?

2. Do you ever say a friendly hello to men first?

3. Do you believe most men only say hello as a way to start flirting?

4. Do you think there's anything in your demeanor that tends to discourage men from speaking to you? For example, an expression on your face that could be interpreted as unfriendly? A curt manner of speech? Unapproachable body language?

Say, Baby, What's Yo' Name?

Ladies, I'm sure there's nothing worse than the uninvited advances of a man. Especially those who approach with overused old pickup lines that they think are clever. I'll bet that every three seconds a woman in the United States is approached by a man who tries to get her phone number using a tired old line. Like a flat tire, there's no good time for such things.

I've compiled a list of the twenty-five most overused, tired, weak pickup lines ever. These are certified and authenticated lines that every woman has been or will be confronted with at some point. These weak lines have been rated in three criteria on an intensity scale of 0–5—0 being the least and 5 being the most intense. The criteria are:

1. **Repulsion Factors**
   a. Yawn Factor: Measures the degree to which the line makes you feel the uncontrollable urge to yawn in the man's face
   b. Scream Factor: Measures the degree of repulsion in terms of how loud you want to scream from insult
   c. Skin Crawl Factor: Measures the degree to which this man makes your skin crawl
2. **Nerve** (the audacity to say such a thing)
3. **Digitability** (given the circumstances, the probability that he can turn that weak opener into getting your phone number).

Although most of these lines guarantee that you will want to forget the man who said them, some of them can legitimately open a conversation if properly executed.

Following the list, there are three scenarios that will teach you how to strategically defend yourself in the face of these attacks by cliché Casanovas. Read these and you'll know how to get rid of every jive-talking man on the face of the earth. This includes everybody from the wannabe sophisticated jerk to the potbellied, cat-calling man on the street corner to the gold-toothed Mr. Jheri Curl.

CATEGORY 1: YOU MUST BE JOKING

This category consists of lines that are such clichés that you think the guy can't be serious. (Repulsion is measured by the Yawn Factor.)

1. "Say, baby, what's yo' name?"
Big yawn. A grown man using leftover lines from high school gets no play.
Yawn Factor—5   Nerve—5   Digitability—0

2. "You need to call me."
He says this as he hands you his business card. This is most likely a wannabe trying to be sophisticated. Although he's faking confidence and control, he's probably a real chump. Chances are the card may not even be from a real business.
Yawn Factor—5   Nerve—5   Digitability—0

3. "Hi."
This one doesn't require much effort and is a good way for a guy to test the water before jumping in. But if

delivered without confidence, it reeks of cowardice. However, many women will let a man stumble through a few more words before bringing the curtain down.
Yawn Factor—4 Nerve—1 Digitability—3

4. "Is someone sitting here?"
This can be a good solid opener. But it gives away the next move like a beginning boxer learning to fake a punch. However, it's a sincere and open approach with several possible conversation spin-offs.
Yawn Factor—4 Nerve—2 Digitability—3

5. "Don't I know you?"
Often followed by the name of a school, group of friends, or place you've never heard of. If you knew this guy, you'd want to forget him anyway. Of course, it might be different if he looked like someone you wanted to remember!
Yawn Factor—5 Nerve—4 Digitability—0

6. "Can we do lunch sometime?"
Here's a man who's coming straight at you without games. He wants to get to know you, and he makes a respectful move. It's a daring approach because he's left wide open.
Yawn Factor—2 Nerve—5 Digitability—4

7. "Are you married?"/"Do you have a boyfriend?"/"I know you have a man."
This is really weak material. It's like conceding before the

battle. If he were more experienced and assertive, he'd just start talking and learn those things through a conversation.
Yawn Factor—4   Nerve—3   Digitability—0

8. "Excuse me. I didn't mean to stare, but you have the prettiest [eyes, skin, hair, dress, etc.]."
Sincere flattery is the best kind of chivalry. The key to this line is honesty and spontaneity. It really helps if he's observant enough to notice something other than your face, rear, or chest.
Yawn Factor—0   Nerve—3   Digitability—4

9. "I'm sorry, I didn't catch your name."
It's no small wonder he didn't catch your name. You never said it! He gets no play.
Yawn Factor—5   Nerve—5+   Digitability—0

10. "Do you come here often?"
This is so clichéd that it has come back around to being a legitimate opener. If immediately followed by some intelligent and witty casual banter, it could be a good icebreaker.
Yawn Factor—4   Nerve—3   Digitability—1

CATEGORY 2: WHAT KIND OF GIRL DO YOU THINK I AM?
These are lines that make you wonder why a man would want a woman who would respond to such crap. (In this section, the Scream Factor is the measure of repulsion.)

11. "I can turn you out."
Spoken by a man who is sure that he's the best Casanova since Don Juan. Guaranteed to turn your stomach.
Scream Factor—5+   Nerve—5   Digitability—0

12. "Whassup?" or "Yo!"
More warmed-over high school material. He gets no conversation.
Scream Factor—5   Nerve—5   Digitability—0

13. "I'm looking for a new secretary."
Stated with a sly grin by a fat and sloppy man who assumes that you'd swap your gym-hardened body to take dictation on his lap.
Scream Factor—5+   Nerve—5+   Digitability—0

14. "What you need is a man like me to take care of you."
Stated in a whisper by somebody who thinks he's a player but doesn't have a pot to piss in or a window to throw it out of.
Scream Factor—5   Nerve—5   Digitability—0

15. "You know I want you, baby."
The problem is that *you* don't want this Jheri-curl-dripping, gold-toothed alien.
Scream Factor—5   Nerve—5   Digitability—0

16. ". . . but are you happily married?"
This man assumes you want to play around and jeopardize

the house, car, and kids to meet him for an hour in a
vibrating water bed at a cheap motel.
Scream Factor—5   Nerve—5   Digitability—0

17. "I would get rid of all of my women for you."
This brother thinks he's the player supreme. You're supposed to be flattered and faint at his feet when you hear
this line.
Scream Factor—5   Nerve—5   Digitability—0

18. "Gimme a chance."/"We need to get to know each
other better."/"How can I get with you?"
Said in shameless begging after another line has been re-
jected. It's usually recited up close to your face with head
and arm movements similar to those used by rappers.
Scream Factor—5   Nerve—5   Digitability—0

19. "Call me on my pager."
Beware of man who will give you his pager number but
won't give you his home phone number. He figures that if
you fall for this one, you're probably naive enough to
swallow the rest of his game.
Scream Factor—4   Nerve—3   Digitability—0

20. "Baby, you're so juicy that I want to sop you up on
some corn bread and lick the plate clean."
It's obvious that this country bumpkin just fell off the
back of a cabbage truck and hit his head. Sadly, this is his
best material, and he's totally serious.
Scream Factor—5   Nerve—3   Digitability—0

CATEGORY 3: ANIMAL SOUNDS, MOANS,
AND GROANS
These lines make you seriously wonder if the man has some
undiscovered mental problems. (In this section, repulsion is
measured by the Skin Crawl Factor.)

21. "Ruff . . . ruff . . . grrrr . . . aoooo."
Enough said.
Skin Crawl Factor—5+   Nerve—5   Digitability—0

22. "Meeeow."
Considering this gentleman probably spends lots of time
practicing, it should be flattering. But it isn't.
Skin Crawl Factor—5   Nerve—5   Digitability—0

23. "Ssssss . . . sssss . . . sssss."
The mating call of the reptile. Often accompanied by an
irritating tug on the arm to get your attention.
Skin Crawl Factor—5+   Nerve—5   Digitability—0

24. "Mmmm, mmmm, mmmm."
This could work if the man has the personality to keep the
situation on a light and humorous level.
Skin Crawl Factor—3   Nerve—3   Digitability—1

25. "Damn!" or "Shit!"
Although words, they're usually mutated into grunts by a
big round-shouldered man with a potbelly calling and
waving at you from a street corner.
Skin Crawl Factor—4   Nerve—4   Digitability—0

HOW TO REPEL UNINVITED CASANOVAS

Some women love the attention of pickup lines. As they turn their heads in disinterest, roll their eyes, or ignore men, they're really reeling in an egotistical celebration. A friend of mine put it all in perspective for me. We were talking when I noticed a glum look on her face.

"What's wrong?" I asked.

She responded with a question: "Do you think I'm pretty?"

"I think you're very pretty."

"But no men tried to talk to me at the mall today," she said with concern.

Funny, she's usually complaining about the nuisance of men trying to flirt with her.

On the other hand, some women complain that men coming on to them makes them feel afraid, embarrassed, even victimized. Fear no more. You can repel weak lines the same way Off! spray repels mosquitoes. Some women have hundreds of one-line comebacks guaranteed to make any man feel two feet tall. But that could trigger aggression from some of the crazy people walking around out there. Some women get stumped and petrified in fear. This causes some men to feel they've captured your interest and you just don't know what to say. I suggest a more strategic and tactical approach. Learn to flow with the situation. Don't anticipate the coming line; feel it, flow with it. It's like tai chi. Relax and use the energy to repel the unwanted man. The following three scenarios will give you a feel for this art:

SCENARIO 1: REPELLING A CATEGORY 1 LINE
(YOU MUST BE JOKING)

For Line 2 ("You need to call me")
You're standing at the bar and waiting for your girlfriend to return from the ladies' room. You hate moments like this. If she doesn't return soon, some man (other than the one you've been eyeing all night) is going to try to sit next to you. Sure enough, a geek (JOE) smiles and lumbers toward you with a sneaky grin on his face. He looks stupid, but you can't tell him he's not as cool as the north wind.

JOE (handing you his business card): You need to call me. My name is Attorney Joe Williams. I've been watching you all night and I want you to know that you're the best-looking lady at this party.

YOU (smiling): Thank you for the compliment. But I can't call you and I don't think I'd better keep your card. You see, my boyfriend is very jealous and obsessive. In fact, that's why he went to the penitentiary . . . the first time. He's an ax murderer due out on parole next month. I'm afraid something terrible may happen to you if he finds your card in my purse.

JOE (blank-faced stare): Oh.

SCENARIO 2: REPELLING A CATEGORY 2 LINE
(WHAT KIND OF GIRL DO YOU THINK I AM?)

For Lines 11 ("I can turn you out"); 12 ("Yo!"); 15 ("You know I want you, baby"); and 17 ("I would get rid of all of my women for you")
At the same party, Mr. Jheri Curl approaches with his eyes fixed on your chest. You cringe. He advances.

MR. JHERI CURL: Yo! You know I want you, baby. I would get rid of all of my women for you.

YOU (acting surprised and flattered by putting your hand over your mouth and popping out your eyes): Really?

MR. JHERI CURL (moving closer to your ear; you can smell his Old Spice cologne mixed with Brut aftershave): I'm kinky, baby. I can turn you out.

YOU: Ooh, I like kinky men. I have this fantasy that I can't get any man to try. But it just makes me tingle to think about it. Do you like to try new things?

MR. JHERI CURL: I'm game, baby. *[smacking his gum]* What is it?

YOU (whispering seductively into his ear): Well . . . I've always wanted to tie a man down to the bed and get him really horny. I'd massage him and tease him with a feather until he couldn't take it and . . .

MR. JHERI CURL: Yeah, I likes this. Then what, baby?

YOU: I would do a striptease act and fling my G-string onto his face. Then, when he starts begging for it . . .

MR. JHERI CURL: Ooh, baby! Whatcha gonna do then?

YOU: Then I'd douse him with gasoline and set him on fire. It would be the ultimate orgasm!

MR. JHERI CURL (almost dropping his drink as he hurries away mumbling to himself): Something's wrong with that sister.

YOU: Hey, where are you going? I'm not finished. I haven't got to the good part yet!

SCENARIO 3: REPELLING A CATEGORY 3 LINE
(ANIMAL SOUNDS, MOANS, AND GROANS)

For Line 21 ("Ruff . . . ruff . . . grrrr . . . aoooo")

Remember, the object in repelling these lines is to flow with the situation. The barking-dog line is supposed to put the man on the aggressive-offensive and you on the passive-defensive. The barker wants you to shrivel up and feel helpless to his advances. Instead, sling off your pumps, drop to all fours, and bark back. Act like a rabid dog, complete with a foaming mouth.

THINGS TO THINK ABOUT

1. How important are opening lines to you?
2. When a man approaches you for the first time, do you judge him primarily by how smooth and clever his conversation is?
3. Do you prefer a man to have a preset opening line or a straightforward approach when meeting you?

I Am More Than Meets the Eye

There are over fifteen million black men in the United States. Each of us is a different book with a different cover. Fraternally we are Freemasons, Shriners, Knights of Columbus, Elks, Alphas, Kappas, Omegas, Sigmas, etc. . . . In the military we storm the beaches as marines, drop from the sky as army rangers, strafe the ground as fighter pilots, and lurk beneath the sea in submarines. In the justice system we are police officers, criminals, prosecutors, defense attorneys, and judges. We heal the sick as physicians, pull teeth as dentists, and perform complex operations as surgeons. In the entrepreneurial world, we are among the risk takers who make this nation's economy turn.

We sell newspapers on the corner, operate hot-dog stands in the park, develop real estate, own insurance companies, clean bathrooms, construct buildings, repair copiers, and manage multimillion-dollar financial portfolios. In the corporate world we occupy positions from mail clerk to boardmember, to chief executive officer. Politically we vary from radical left to conservative right to dead center. Sexually we're straight, bisexual, and gay. When we're happy, we shout. When we're hurt, we cry. When we bleed, the blood is red. In short, we are no different from any other group of Americans.

I thank God that I grew up with strong positive images of black men. Otherwise I might have believed some of the negative hype about us. I grew up seeing black men in the roles of entrepreneurs, physicians, Ph.D.s, lawyers, and skilled laborers. In fact, as a boy, for a long time I thought it was mostly blacks who owned Mercedes, Jaguars, and BMWs because blacks were the only people I saw driving them. The problem I encountered wasn't trying to find a good role model. Rather, it was trying to understand why all the rest of the world didn't share the positive image of black men that I had.

Needless to say, as I got older, I didn't just bump into the stereotypes about black men—I slammed into them head-on. One of my most poignant encounters with overt racism happened in high school. One day my trusty old Honda Civic was in the shop for some engine work. My mother wasn't feeling well that morning and couldn't drop me off, so she let me take her car to school. I didn't really think much of it when I pulled into the parking lot in my mother's Mercedes. But it turned some heads; in particular, the head of a white guy whom I'd considered a friend. He watched me park and then he whisked his little sports car over next to me. He turned down his blasting rock music and yelled, "Where did you steal that car, nigger?" He burst into laughter. But his sidekick looked afraid. He must have been reading the expression on my face. Point-blank rage.

That was the wrong time in my life for someone to say something like that to me. I hadn't developed much patience or ability to think through anger. I wanted to do something to hurt him and salvage my ego. I don't remember how long it took for me to respond. It was probably all of three seconds. Before I knew what I was doing, I was standing at his window with an A&W root beer in my hand. I slammed it into his face. Then I shook the can and opened it. It exploded all over the pristine interior of his car. I turned the can upside down to make sure I got every drop. Then I crushed the can with my hand and dropped it in his lap. He wasn't laughing anymore. And now his sidekick was laughing at him.

That was my crash course in stereotypes of black men. A course that every black man, and black woman for that matter, must take to survive in this society. The lesson I learned is that there are people in this world who have their minds narrowly focused on skin color. Ironically, I was also painfully aware that such a mentality existed among African Americans. Our own skin-color consciousness and social-class segregation was just as painful and real to me as being called a "nigger" by a white guy.

However, the root-beer incident was more than my indoctrination to the world of racism. It gave me a new and different perspective. It showed me the true face of racism. My friend felt threatened because I had something nice. That's why he attacked me. Because I felt threatened, I counterattacked. We have the same cycle played out every day on a larger scale in our world between different ethnic groups, religions, and governments. Fear is at the root of prejudice.

I was an impetuous teen, and my first reaction to that fear was rage. I was angry that people were forming unfair opinions about me and other black men. Couldn't they see the majesty and grace of black men as clearly as I? Didn't they know who we were? Why couldn't we rise above the ignorance of stereotypes for just one moment? Those questions burned inside me. They eventually came to be my angle on any and every issue. For many years, as far as I was concerned, everything was a black thing.

For a short while, I was content with my rage. Actually, I had even become somewhat of a racist myself. I was on a mission to prove that blacks were superior beings to everyone else on earth, especially whites. But my rage went further than that. For a while I didn't even like light-skinned black people. I viewed them as something less than true African Americans. But deep down I wasn't comfortable with these hostile feelings. For one thing, I had a rainbow of good friends who were all shades of black, white Anglo-Saxon Protestants, Jews, various Euroethnics, Latinos, Asians, and even an exchange student from Norway. Even though the root-beer incident was still eating away at me, I realized I couldn't continue to hold on to my anger. It just wasn't practical.

Eventually I grew out of the rage, and it tempered into a more constructive plan. I decided I would become a crusader for black causes. The same fervent resolve was there. But now it was constructive. I decided to take a positive approach. During my twenties I set out to become the super "race man." I studied my African and African American heritage. I spent hours shopping in black bookstores and black art galleries. I read the great black authors. I took time to learn about black cultures throughout the diaspora. I wanted to absorb everything black that I could.

After spending my life in predominantly white schools, I now chose to attend a black institution, Texas Southern University. During college I worked in my family's business and then started one of my own. I became active in the community and in politics. All to be the best black man that I could be. After earning my degree, I decided that I wanted to jump full throttle into my life as super race man. I had things to do. I had a race to uphold and I didn't feel like sitting through another degree, so I kissed the idea of law school goodbye. I enjoyed my life as an entrepreneur, but I wanted a more direct role in my black community. That's when I decided to run for the state legislature. But it didn't take me long to grow tired of the politics of politics. I then decided that to be the super race man I knew I could be, I needed to be on the front line. I became a police officer. But I still didn't feel as though I was doing all I could do for the black community. I quickly left law enforcement and returned to my family's business. It sounds haphazard, but this zigzag path was leading me to spiritual enlightenment.

It was that chain of events which prompted me to start writing again. I had enjoyed writing as a child, but it had been years since I had written anything. But I felt a calling to do it. I decided that the best way to be super race man was to be a race writer. As a writer I'd be unencumbered and free to speak my mind. For a few years I cranked out articles for different black magazines. My theme was uplifting messages intended exclusively for black people. But the more I delved into the exercise of writing messages with positive themes for black people, the more spiritually attuned I became. The more spiritual I became, the more I realized the universal value of what I was saying. I started seeing myself as connected not only to those who looked like me but to the rest of the world too.

That was an unwanted and initially troubling quantum shift in my life. It reminds me of when God knocked the apostle Paul off his horse to awaken him to his new destiny. Through my own written words, I realized that my studies of things black and African had led me to a conclusion I wasn't prepared for: that the ultimate answers to my life as a black man wouldn't be found exclusively in my blackness. The answers were in my soul. The part of me that was bigger than my color. Raising consciousness among blacks was a noble thing. But it didn't stop there. This was not a lessening of my black consciousness, but a new affirmation of my humanity.

Then came the hard part. The next step on the journey was

the construction of a bridge from my world as a black man to the world around me. Reaching out not only to my people but to other people as well, I went from trying to be a super race man to trying to be a good man. That changed my entire outlook on life.

Initially I fought this feeling. But when something is right it's like fire. It burns, pierces, melts, and peels away what's there and transforms it into something more basic and pure. I started to see that the struggles of black men and the black community were the same as the struggles of any oppressed people throughout the history of the world, whether they had black skin or not. And the struggles of any oppressed people were the problems of everyone, including the majority. That's because no society can sustain itself successfully for long with oppression and prejudice at its roots. Nor can the world as a whole. At that point I started to feel a connection with anyone who was part of the universal energy force, whether they looked like me or not.

I have found that the common denominator linking black people or any other human being to the world is our spirits. We are all children of the same creator. We are all spirits on a journey through this world that will eventually return us to the source, where we are one. Those things were revealed to me after I worked through my rage. Now I have a better perspective. Although many people may only see my black skin when they look at me, that's their problem. I know that I am more than meets the eye.

THINGS TO THINK ABOUT

1. What was your most poignant encounter with racism?

2. Have you developed a constructive way to handle the prejudices of people you encounter?

3. Have you identified your own prejudices?

4. Are you allowing a focus on racism to limit your spiritual growth?

5. Have you considered the universal spiritual aspect of your existence and how it relates to the entire world?

What Is a Good Brother?

Here's a pop quiz. Identify the "good brothers" among the following choices:

A. Terrel is twenty-three, single, and has a two-year-old son. Terrel's a rugged character with a clean bald fade. He proudly pays his rent to a black landlord in a predominantly black section of urban Houston known as the Third Ward. He's also employed at a small restaurant in that community. After his day shift there, he walks a few blocks to the community college, where he's studying to earn a certificate in computer networking. Later, after getting a job in the industry, he plans to earn a bachelor's degree in computer science. He openly expresses love for all things black: art, literature, dark-toned women . . . But despite carrying a photo of his son in his wallet and bragging about him at every chance, he rarely pays his child support.

B. Malik is thirty-five, married, and has one child. As a well-known expert on Afrocentricity, he has written several books and is in constant demand on the lecture circuit. He never hesitates to be at the forefront of issues concerning blacks. Most recently, he spearheaded a losing battle to prevent his employer from abolishing affirmative action. He is the chairman of the African American studies department at a predominantly white university.

C. Brian is a thirty-nine-year-old entrepreneur, divorced, with no children. After being passed over for a promotion twice, he left corporate America to start his own business. Being on his own wasn't easy. His first three years were a constant struggle. He almost lost everything trying to make his

dream come true. But finally he was starting to reap the benefits of his work. Things had been good for the past few years.
He was able to buy a home in the suburbs. His wardrobe was
finally getting some pizazz. And he bought a new Jeep Chero-
kee. He also asked his girlfriend to marry him. She's a petite
Asian woman he'd been dating for almost two years.

D. Jason is forty-three, married, and has two children. He is
a graduate of Stanford University, where he was president of
his black fraternity. After graduation, he went to law school at
Yale. Currently he's a partner in a large and well-respected San
Francisco firm. He's active in several community groups, especially the local branch of the Republican Party.

E. Jeffrey, aka "Slam," is a twenty-three-year-old basketball
millionaire straight from the South Side of Chicago. If it
weren't for a basketball scholarship he wouldn't have made it
out of his tough neighborhood. But he's quick to point out that
he's not a slave to the NBA or the team's owner. He's angry at
reporters for what he feels is unfair coverage of him, coverage
he says makes him seem overaggressive and violent just because
he doesn't take what the "man" dishes out. He has been fined
for things he's said both on and off the court. Slam says he's
just a proud black man whom the system is trying to control.
He makes it a policy to date only black women. But he is noted
as having a collection of black women that covers the entire
United States. None of which are more than bedroom toys to
him.

Which one is a good brother, the most authentic black man?

I suppose at first glance some people would say Terrel is the
most authentic black man of all the choices. But how can he
plan his future in such a detailed manner and not even take care
of his child support payments? Next, I suppose many would
consider Malik the most authentic of all the choices. But if he is

so Afrocentric, why is he on the faculty of a predominantly white university? Brian sounds like a good man to be held out as an example. But can he be a good brother if he doesn't live in the hood and dates a woman outside his ethnic group? Jason seems like an example of a good brother. But he's a Republican. Can he be a good brother and wear the Republican elephant on his lapel? Last there's Slam. He calls black women Nubian queens. But if he really felt they were queens, would he be using them as toys?

I pose these examples to make a point. The black male has been robbed of his God-granted individualism by stereotypes imposed on us by the majority culture and by those within our own culture as well. Otherwise it wouldn't be necessary to raise the question of what a good brother is or whether a black man is a "credit to his race." Have you ever heard anyone say, "Now there's a white man who's a credit to his race"? Hardly. White males don't have their identity questioned at every turn and by everyone. They're allowed to make individual decisions and still continue to be white men.

However, black men are almost always assessed by the way they look. But the black male is a book that can't be judged by its cover. We have personalities, philosophies, and thoughts, just like everyone else, that aren't detectable in a quick glance. Unfortunately, not many people look beyond our skin color to find out who we really are and what we're all about. Not only is the majority culture guilty of this; blacks are too. Somewhere along the rocky road to liberating our minds we have developed a mixed signal of conformity and individualism. African Americans say we have the same rights as any other people on earth. But then we seriously limit ourselves by enforcing unspoken rules and parameters for what black male individualism can and should be.

A major reason for the loss of individuality in black males is the lack of role models available to many young black men. Most of the role model images offered to young black men are those of athletes, entertainers, and politicians. Young black men generally don't get much exposure to the "ordinary heroes": doctors, lawyers, teachers, scientists, entrepreneurs, police officers, firefighters, paramedics, skilled laborers, etc. It's not as though these men don't exist. There are plenty of ordinary black heroes out there. They just aren't put in the spotlight very often. Without a supply of tangible role models, young black males grow up with a skewed vision of all they can be. They start thinking that if they can't play ball, act, rap, or be a great political figure, there's nothing else they can aspire to. This lack of diversity then becomes self-limiting. Without seeing enough options, many young black men conform to warped views of what being a good brother should be. Often the following distortions of black manhood are the only role models available to many young black men.

ANGRY BLACK MAN
Sometimes we misconstrue expressions of anger as expressions of pride. For some black men, being a good brother equals being angry and rebellious against all things of the majority culture. While any black man or woman can relate to the legitimate pain that creates the source of that anger, the anger itself doesn't do anything but work to destroy the individual.

DASHIKI CHIC
This is the belief that ethnic clothing makes a black man a good brother. But sporting a Kente necktie at a public function doesn't bring you any closer to your African heritage. Wearing

a dashiki doesn't make you more of a good brother than a black man in a suit. Anybody can go out and buy African clothing.

TALKIN' THE TALK
Knowing the current slang terms and how to give the latest soul grip is what some black men consider being a good brother. But the way you speak doesn't make you a good brother. Neither does mastery of complicated handshakes.

BEING A PLAYER
Collecting women is the meaning of manhood for too many men, black and otherwise. The player feels that his worth as a man is determined by the number of women he can influence and control. The player sees women as conquests, a test for his manhood. The question he asks himself when he sees an attractive woman is "Can I get her?" Underlying that question is the belief that if he can seduce this woman into bed, it says something about his manliness. In essence, the player's manhood is based on a delicately balanced ego and a warped sense of values.

THE PERSONAL IS POLITICAL
There are brothers who feel that always looking for the black political angle is an indication of how black they are. But political issues are often a complex mixture of issues, of which race may only be one factor. Many political issues are about race, but not all of them are. Attempting to view every political issue in terms of race can be a mistake. Also, supporting a candidate simply because he or she is black isn't necessarily the right choice. Nor does being a Democrat make you more black than a black Republican.

TOO COOL

This is the idea that to be a good brother is to be cool. It is a stereotype of black men and unfortunately many try to live it. The cool brother is a master of style. His character is built upon his car, collection of fine clothing, and smoothness with words. He loves parties and nightclubs; that's where he has a chance to style and profile, his favorite activity. There's little depth beyond the cool brother's exterior because he's primarily interested in looking good. Cool brothers are also usually womanizers.

CAN YOU TELL A GOOD BROTHER FROM A FAKE?

In examining the question of what a "good brother" is I inevitably came around to considering myself. The first time we all shouted "Run, Jesse, run," I was only eighteen, the ink barely dry on my voter's registration card. But I was a Jackson delegate all the way to the state Democratic convention. I'm a member of the Prince Hall Masons, a historically black Masonic lodge. I have a degree in business from Texas Southern University, a historically black college. I teach creative writing classes to kids in inner-city schools. I live in a black neighborhood and vote in a predominantly black political district. I'm respectful to black women. Sounds good on paper. But none of those things automatically qualifies me as a good brother.

External things don't make me a good brother. The qualities inside are what make me the man I am (see the chapter "I Am More Than Meets the Eye"). But often people don't look beyond the exterior of black men to see their interior qualities, not even blacks. Often blacks stereotype black men too. And this black-on-black stereotyping is even more damaging than stereotyping by the majority culture. This is because black-on-black stereotypes more directly affect the views and opinions we have of ourselves; they even have an impact on what we teach black children. But instead of issuing stereotypes about ourselves, we need to send out the message in our community that being a "good brother" is based on a man's character and not external things.

Take Tony Brown and Charles Barkley, for example. They are two black men who dare to be different on the exterior but are still authentic black men. Journalist Tony Brown is a Republican. But he's also one of the most outspoken champions of black political and economic issues. Basketball superstar Charles Barkley married a woman outside his ethnic group. But I don't think anybody could call him a quiet Uncle Tom pandering to the whims of white America. Those two men don't fit the typical "black man" mold, but they are unquestionably authentic black men.

Being a good brother isn't defined by how well you fit a stereotypical mold determined by what you look like or seem to be. It's when you're doing things that are blessings to your life and thus the lives of those around you. These aren't outer things, but inner things. It isn't your achievements, your politics, or your clothing that makes you a good brother. We've all seen those items flaunted and fronted in counterfeit. Instead it's the small things that make your life and the lives of others better. Nobody can tell you when you reach this point. Awards and honors don't put you there. Being a good brother is knowing who you are, where you are, and where you're going. It's being walking, talking, positive energy.

By the way, if you chose any of the men in the pop quiz, you answered both correctly and incorrectly. No doubt, all are black men. Like any other human beings, they have good points and flaws. Reclaiming our God-given right to be considered full human beings means we have the right to have who we are as people take precedence over our skin color, not the other way around. No brother is more authentically black than any other solely on the basis of external characteristics. Deborah Mathis put this issue in focus in her essay "Ghettocentrism," from the anthology of black journalists *Thinking Black:* ". . . the so-called black experience is not singular or one-dimensional but capable of many forms. We do not live, think, or thrive the same way, or on the same things. Yet, none are spared racial discrimination. Somehow, it always finds us, rendering the 'search for authenticity' an absurdity. Every black experience is the real thing."

Being a "good brother" has nothing to do with the clothes you wear, your attitude, your woman, or how angry you are at the "man." Being a good brother translates into being an authentic man. A real man is a benefit to himself, his family, his community, his city, his state, his country, his world, his universe . . . to God. Galatians 5:22 states that the fruits of spirit are "love, joy, peace, patience, kindness, goodness, faithfulness, gentleness, and self-control." That is the definition of a good brother. A tree bearing spiritual fruit for all to enjoy.

POINTS TO REMEMBER

- Being a good brother isn't limited to any particular attitude, clothing, vocabulary, or personal politics. It certainly isn't about being cool or womanizing.
- One can't determine whether a black man is a good brother merely by his physical appearance.
- Good brothers come in a variety of looks, personalities, and personal styles.
- A good brother is a benefit not only to blacks but to everyone.
- Young black men need a wide variety of role models, not just athletes, entertainers, and politicians. Often the best role models are hardworking "ordinary heroes."

A Lesson in True Manhood

We snorted like bulls as we paced inside the circle of screaming kids. We eyed each other intensely. The first one to blink would be the first one to get hit. The crowd around us was livid. They wanted to see two of the largest boys in the fourth grade fight. The fact that we were best friends seemed to make the crowd even more excited. It felt as though something in them wanted our friendship torn apart. The entire scene felt evil. But still I was prepared to fight. Too puffed up with pride to back away.

I remember hearing an excited voice yell, "Billy and Charles are having a fight!" Then one of the more aggressive hecklers shoved Charles at me. I felt two hands grab my shoulders from behind and lunge me forward. Charles and I collided and began a shoulder-to-shoulder shoving match as we walked in a circle. Then our eyes locked again. I couldn't believe it. I was about to brawl with my best friend. I couldn't even remember why we were fighting. I just knew there was no turning back. The crowd had grown larger and more aggressive. If we didn't fight now, they'd jump on us for disappointing them.

We continued to make circles in the dust. But I could feel that we were moments away from throwing punches. That was when the ugliness of the whole thing completely set in on me. Between one of the shoves, several seconds stretched out into what felt like an hour. It was then that I had enough time to realize what was really going on. It was a collision of good and

evil. Darkness was looming over our friendship, and we had to
fight it with the light of wisdom and love. It was in that instant
that I became deflated and humble.

Suddenly, I felt my face pucker. Then my eyes were heavy
with water. I squinted to hold back the inevitable. But they
came. A flood of tears burst out of my eyes and washed down
my cheeks. But I continued to act as though I was going to
fight. More tears came, a rush that started deep in my heart,
welled up in my chest, and escaped from my eyes. I loved
Charles. He was my best friend. I didn't want to fight him and
I wasn't going to do it. I was even prepared to fight the agita-
tors in the crowd if that's what I had to do to avoid this. But I
wasn't going to fight him. I'd made up my mind.

But instead of closing in on us, the kids started laughing at
me and the crowd started to break up. Relief filled me. With
all my heart I didn't want to fight Charles. For me the tears
were worth preventing the end of a great friendship. But a
small stinging part of me felt ashamed. I had cried in a fight.
Lost by default. Now I would have to live with that every day at
school. I was only a half a block from home, but it was going to
be a long and lonely walk.

I was drying my tears and picking up my books when
Charles walked over and gave me a hug. He didn't want to
fight either. His gesture was one of true friendship. Although
not one blow was thrown, we did in fact have a big fight. We
fought the internal battle of good versus evil. We had chosen
light over darkness and were ready to accept the difficult challenges brought on by such a decision. Something more difficult
to do than throwing fists.

What Charles did that day saved what has become a lifelong
friendship. As a ten-year-old boy he had the courage to do what

so many grown men can't do. Give a hug instead of a fist. He had the strength. No adult was around to force us to make up. He didn't have to do it. He passed me positive energy and it felt good to my spirit. A hug of reconciliation is warm and big. It returns a part of you that you had felt was lost. A part that you had feared you would have trouble healing. But when the other person brings it back to you, it's like a ball of glowing energy. It instantly perks you up. That's good love. The kind that lifts you and makes your life better.

I learned that day that avoiding a fight doesn't mean you're not a strong man. On the contrary, it shows that you are strong because you have the internal fortitude to solve things by other means. Too many men associate strength and masculinity with shouting, gnashing of teeth, balled fists, and guns. Exploding to show their displeasure rather than developing the temperament to come to cool conclusions. But exploding isn't masculinity. It's fear. Fear acted out in the same way a frightened dog bites. Fear thriving through the body and soul of a man who has not claimed control of himself.

I'm not advocating that a man stand still and get beaten to the ground. Self-defense is a different story. Self-defense deflects negative energy back to its source. I call it giving somebody an energy adjustment, because self-defense is not destructive in and of itself. When I was a police officer, I quickly learned the difference between self-defense and fear-based aggression. Self-defense is fighting to the degree necessary to eliminate a threat. And no further than that. That is totally different from fear-based aggression, which is the violent explosion of a person who feels threatened because of their own fears and insecurities. Examples of fear-based aggression include: racism, sexism, ageism, homophobia, religious persecution, gang banging, etc. This sort of aggression has no boundaries.

One of the greatest warriors of all times was Sun Tzu. His wisdom about the art of conflict was recorded in his timeless book *The Art of War*. Ironically, he believed physical conflict was to be avoided if at all possible. Sun Tzu's dictum was "To win without fighting is best." One of history's wisest warriors warned us to avoid the destructive rages of violence. Why haven't we learned this yet?

The stronger man is the one who does not explode in anger. The greater man is the one who has the power to overcome his enemy by exercising the power to control himself. His wisdom will take him much further in life than someone who carries his manhood in a clenched fist. This is a valuable lesson that boys need to learn when they are young, a lesson that may save them from an untimely death brought on by a gun or knife. Knowing that the ultimate power is self-control will undoubtedly save lots of guys from hearing the penitentiary gate slamming closed on them for twenty years to life.

Physical power is not a bad thing in and of itself. Nor is it the total measure of manhood. The interior strength is what controls it all. Without interior controls, there's not much of a man, only unfocused energy whirling around, threatening to destroy itself and anything in its path. To be a real man, a man must gain the spiritual power to regulate his physical actions. This will assure that he walks in the light of wisdom.

That wisdom shielded us from the rumors of the fight that beat us to school the next day. The mob had created their own stories. Some said Charles whipped me so bad that I started crying and ran home. Some said I was so angry that I cried and whipped Charles to the ground. I don't remember hearing the actual truth in any of the rumors, the story that said there had been no fight. The only story was a truly manly hug between Charles and me. Two boys who took a giant step toward being real men. And I'm glad it turned out that way. We're still the best of friends today. And better men for it.

THINGS TO THINK ABOUT

1. Have you found ways to constructively deal with your own anger, rage, or frustration?

2. Can you remember a time when you said or did something out of anger that you later wished you hadn't? What happened as a result?

3. Do you make it a point to make peace with someone you love after an argument?

4. What are some things we can teach children about the nonviolent resolution of disagreements?

I Need Your Respect

Respect isn't just something all people want. It's a basic human need. It's something people will negotiate, fight, and even kill for. It was a song for Aretha Franklin. It was the punch line of a joke that made comedian Rodney Dangerfield rich and famous. But for black men it's no song, and it sure as hell isn't a joke. For every black man, getting just basic human respect can sometimes be elusive and is not guaranteed.

I realize that daily life is a battle for everyone, not just for the black male. Under the universal pressures of hectic work schedules, bill collectors calling, and relationships falling apart, black men are not the only people in America feeling psychologically squeezed. Today everyone is complaining about the difficulty of holding it all together.

But as a black male, I don't just fight the common daily battles of life. There's another dimension to my existence. Black men are locked into a struggle for respect and self-affirmation in a society that sometimes views us more as myth and stereotype than as human being. That's a hard role to deal with. A role that threatens to make me self-conscious at times, be it actively or passively manifested. Unfortunately, some people dismiss such thinking as black male paranoia.

But for me it's just reality. Every moment of every day I have to wonder about the dual meaning of the smallest gesture or word. Sometimes I even avoid going to places where I will be conspicuous because I don't want to be looked at and studied like an animal in the zoo. Sometimes I avoid certain areas of my own city because I know my very blackness will be viewed suspiciously and I will draw too much attention. Being a black male can affect my decisions about where I go, when I go, what I do, and what I wear. But sometimes all the strategic planning gets to me. That's when I become so fed up that I wear whatever I want and go wherever I want, and say, "To hell with letting the prejudices and problems of others cage me in."

That's because it really doesn't matter how I'm dressed or what I look like. My mere presence can evoke fear and hostility in some people. I can walk across the street in a suit with an attaché case in hand and still be subjected to the clicks of doors locking, windows rolling up, and horrified faces who immediately take me to be nothing more than a well-dressed car-jacker approaching to seize their BMW or Cadillac. Once, as I shopped in a mall, a lady clutched her infant's hand and froze until I passed. What was she afraid of? The only lethal weapon I had was an American Express Gold Card.

I recall handing a twenty-dollar bill to a deli cashier to pay for my lunch. Without a word or hesitation, he held it up to the light to see if it was counterfeit. Sure, in his job he probably routinely scrutinizes money. But I detected an air of contempt when he did it to me. Then there was the time an alarm went off as a white woman and I exited a record store at the same moment. Guess whose bag they wanted to check? Those situations probably wouldn't have been so disturbing had they not been the continuation of an old, familiar pattern, a pattern of blatant disrespect.

It might be a joke when comedian Rodney Dangerfield delivers his famous old line about getting "no respect." But it's no joke to black men. There's not a damn thing funny about what feels like an organized effort to assassinate our manhood. Some older black men who have survived and thrived in spite of it all will shrug their shoulders at the problem and rationalize it away. Meanwhile their silent frustration eats away at their insides. In contrast, the young disenfranchised black men on the streets are far more volatile. Sadly, they demand respect even if it is gained by extreme costs to others or themselves. For so many of them, respect is achieved by a finger on a trigger, a knife, or balled fist. Those young brothers vividly illustrate the fact that getting respect is no joke to any of us.

Click on the television talk shows and you'll see a painful reminder of this disrespect. On too many such shows you can find a familiar guest who is a ratings booster. Instead of featuring one of the many proud and articulate black women who don't subscribe to stereotypes about black men, the producers intentionally choose the neck-jerking, eye-rolling, razor-tongued, venomous girl to spit at every black man in the universe. She disrespectfully explains her point that black men are sorry, lazy, and good for nothing. Then they show the man she's angry with. He's a young black male who I suppose we are to believe represents all black men in some way or other. Slouching in a chair with his hand over his mouth and gold chains draped around his neck, he occasionally grunts a word in chopped slang. The audience hisses in disgust.

We expect such inflammation from the media. But black women should be careful not to be duped into leading the charge.

Black women can use their eloquence to propel a man to great heights or knock him down to nothing. "You're just a typical lazy-ass black man." Those are stinging words. Nobody can tongue-lash like an angry black woman. Hell hath no fury like an angry sister! No doubt some black men deserve the harsh words they get. But not all of us. What good is all the finger-pointing and cussing? At some point we need to stop pushing apart and start working together.

Likewise, we as black men must reciprocate the respect we

want from black women. We must also respect ourselves if we want black women to respect us. Respect is a two-way street. It means that if you have children, you need to pay your child support and be a father. If you're drowning in malt liquor, you need to drop the bottle in the trash. If you're gang-banging, you need to throw the gun away. That's where the respect starts, in each man's life. If you respect yourself, then women will find it natural to respect and admire you too.

By using the word "respect," I'm not suggesting that black women kneel down and wash our feet in silent servitude. I'm simply appealing to them to understand that they can be a means of healing for black men. Healing the wounds between black men and women will bring about soul regeneration and affirmation. Our minds need to be at peace with each other in all our ways of interaction, be we friends, lovers, or strangers. We need a mutuality of compassion and understanding. It all begins with a little respect.

THINGS TO THINK ABOUT

1. What can black men do to achieve more respect in society?
2. What must black men do to assure the respect of black women?
3. How can black women help black men attain more respect in society?
4. What can you do in your life to heal the wounds of black men being disrespected in this society?

When You Can't
Take It Anymore

I admit it, I lost my cool. I blew my top.

As I remember it, I was having a bad day. Actually it was a bad day at the end of a bad week, capping off a bad month. It was a time in my life in which I was under too much pressure. By day, I was a police officer running a radar on the freeway. By night and on my off days, I worked in real estate with my family. Basically I was holding down two full-time careers at once. It seemed I was always working. Most days I barely had time to sit down and eat a good meal; I wasn't getting much sleep either. And I didn't have time or energy for much of a social life; I was usually too tired to go out or even talk on the phone for very long. And having off days on Wednesday and Thursday didn't help my social life either.

The day I exploded was one of those times when nothing seemed to go right. I'd worked every night and all day on both my off days for the past week putting together a real estate deal for a buyer and seller who had proven to be two of the most difficult people I'd ever dealt with. But now I'd come to the point at which I had finally got them connected in a deal. I worked all day to put the final touches on the paperwork so I'd have no problem getting their signatures. Meanwhile, the nervous seller was waiting at his office for me to fax him a draft of the contract.

Finally, the last sheet of the contract eased its way out of the printer. I assembled all the papers and put them in the fax machine. I'd had trouble with this fax machine before; it had a bad habit of jamming and misfeeding papers if they weren't put in right, and that was part luck and part practice. When I heard the fax tone, I felt relieved, I was finally finished. But no sooner than the relief filled me, panic drained me. My fax machine was misfeeding the paper, sending them all through at once. I was able to pull out all the papers before they jammed in the fax, but I tore two sheets in the effort.

I reprinted the torn pages and tried to fax the contract again. This time all the pages went through. But then I got a call from my client, he was agitated because the fax was blurred. So I tried to fax again. The fax misfed the paper again and all the pages started going through at once. Again I tore a couple of pages while pulling them out. That's when I lost it. I just couldn't take it anymore. I ripped the fax out of the wall, slammed it on the floor, and stomped on it with my Texas-size boots. Within seconds the fax machine was a crumple of broken plastic. I felt a little better, but I hadn't solved anything. Now I didn't even have a fax to send the contract.

The next thing I knew I was waiting in line at Office Depot with a fax machine under my arm. My tantrum had been a costly lesson in self-control. At this point, I'd blown my deadline and almost five hundred dollars on a new fax machine. That incident seems funny when I look back on it. But when some men vent their frustration, it isn't funny at all, it's dangerous. Some men under pressure don't take it out on stubborn fax machines; they punch out car windows, put fists through walls, or take it out on wives, children, or animals.

For more on men who are dangerous when angry, see the chapter "Domestic Violence: Don't Be a Victim."

But not all men who occasionally experience a need to vent their emotion are dangerous. Both men and women have to vent sometimes. As long as we don't hurt anybody, harm ourselves, or damage valuable property, it's just a harmless outlet for some mental steam, a way of coping with the overload of daily frustration and pressure we all feel in our fast-paced world. When deadlines, screaming supervisors, bills, family problems, house payments, and car payments converge in the mind, it can be too much to handle. My rage wasn't really about the fax machine; it was the accumulation of many things. The fax was just the thing that sent me over the top. I think Nathan McCall said it best with the title of his first book; it all just "makes me wanna holler."

And sometimes I do holler. I roll up the windows in the car and belt a roar as I drive down the street. It helps. I can feel the tension break up in my chest and relax in my neck and shoulders, but that's not always enough. A man can't always yell out his frustrations. Sometimes our minds are so pressured and full of mental clutter from this world that a holler won't help. That's when we need some help handling it all.

But for so long, it hasn't been manly to ask for help. Men have been taught to hold it all inside; not to scream, not to say "I can't handle it," and certainly not to cry. But the result of all that is a toxic mixture of frustration and anger. It's that mixture that opens the door to alcoholism, drug abuse, womanizing, and other self-destructive behaviors some men resort to for mental relief.

Men need to know it's all right to feel overwhelmed, that the measure of their manhood isn't how much pressure they can handle without help. For a long time, men have neglected to share many of their intimate feelings with other people. But the time has come for men to use their relationships for emotional support. That's what friends and family are for. There's nothing wrong with needing to talk to someone. Men need to learn how to reach out for help before they feel the need to explode. Men need to develop deep relationships in which they feel comfortable talking about their feelings, fears, and anxieties.

But sometimes talking to friends and family isn't the best idea. Friends and family often have already formed opinions about us. They see us as a brother, son, father, husband, boyfriend, or best friend. Because of their familiarity with us, they sometimes aren't the best people for us to vent frustrations to. In fact, sometimes they can be part of what's frustrating us. At those times, we need to talk to someone who isn't in our immediate circle of acquaintances, a person with whom we can talk without being seen in a predefined role.

That's when a therapist can be a valuable tool. After I stomped the fax machine, I knew I wasn't handling the pressure I was under as well as I thought I was. Not long after that, I went to a therapist so I could get a few things off my chest. We talked about lots of things, most of which had to do with the overwhelming pressures I felt at the time. Like most men, I was apprehensive about seeing a therapist, but the visit wasn't what I thought it would be. I didn't lie down on a couch and answer questions. I sat in a comfortable chair and we had a casual chat about the subjects that concerned me. I actually enjoyed the one-hour talk. We even laughed quite a bit. It was painless and I felt a great relief afterward.

I'm not ashamed that I went to a therapist and I'll go to a therapist again if I ever feel the necessity. It's far better to vent pain and frustration to a therapist than it is to allow those feelings to erode your emotional health to the point that you would engage in self-destructive habits. And that's the step we need to take as men. We need to accept that we can't always handle everything. We need to reach out to someone when we feel that we just can't take it anymore. When you feel you're at the breaking point, start by talking to a friend or family member. But if it's something you'd rather not (or can't) discuss with a friend or family member, don't hold it in; see a therapist or a minister and get it off your chest. Whether you choose to go to a therapist or a counselor associated with your religious faith, here are some things you might want to consider.

THINGS MEN HOLD IN THAT BUILD UP PRESSURE

- The current state of your relationship
- A recent or past relationship breakup
- Sexual problems
- Issues from your childhood or family issues from the past
- Career problems, loss of a job or being laid off
- Health problems
- Coping with the accumulation of life's pressures
- Anxiety about your financial situation
- Death of loved one or close friend
- Special pressures that you feel as an African American male

WAYS TO EASE YOUR TENSION

- Take time to talk with your male friends. Extend the conversations beyond sports and women. Get into your feelings. Share your feelings and benefit from the kind of healing and therapy that can only come from a good friend (or friends).
- Realize that you're not alone in feeling overwhelmed by pressure; other men feel the same way. Start an informal group of men that get together to network,

mingle, and talk on a regular basis. Don't have an agenda, just shoot baskets, play cards, or eat pizza.

- Seek counseling when you need to talk to a person who has no bias about you and will not judge the things you tell them.
- If possible, take a day off from work to relax your mind, chill out. Minds need rest just as bodies do.
- Get a massage.
- Enjoy some "quiet time." Meditate and pray in silence. Or turn out the lights and put on some soft music.
- Go into an empty room or roll up the windows in your car and HOLLER!

A SPECIAL WORD TO BROTHERS ON SEEKING THERAPY

When selecting a therapist, one needs to check credentials closely to make sure the therapist is properly licensed, qualified, and experienced to handle the intimate details of your life. A competent professional will welcome your questions about their credentials and qualifications. In addition to the general qualifications of a therapist, you may want to seek a therapist who is within your religious faith, or at least is capable of understanding your faith and how it is important to your life.

There is also another important consideration for African American men when hiring a therapist. Is this therapist able to understand the specific set of circumstances you deal with as an African American male? Modern psychology is finally recognizing the necessity for culture-specific therapy. But that doesn't mean all therapists are capable of providing culture-specific therapy. Perhaps you will want an African American male as a therapist. Or maybe the gender and ethnicity of your therapist doesn't matter to you. Whether you choose a psychologist, psychiatrist, or pastoral counselor, select a therapist who can understand your unique life as an African American male.

POINTS TO REMEMBER

- There's no shame in feeling overwhelmed by life's pressures.
- Holding all your pressures and problems inside is not a sign of being manly.
- Holding all your pressures and stress inside can lead to mental and physical illness, alcoholism, and drug abuse.
- Cultivate a nonbusiness activity that gets you together with other men on a regular basis.
- Find a diversion that gets you into a different environment and mind-set, away from the daily routine. Activities such as basketball, softball, bowling, bicycling, tinkering with cars, cooking, sketching, and reading are some good examples.
- Seek more emotional exchange from your friendships with other men.
- If you seek therapy, choose a therapist who can relate to your experiences and feelings as an African American male.

Your Baby's Father or Me?

I don't have anything against dating women with kids. At least half of the women I've dated have kids. It's not an unusual situation to encounter. But I have to confess that I keep my guard up until I check things out. Experience has taught me that just because the father isn't in the house anymore (if he ever was) doesn't mean that he isn't in the picture. When a woman starts talking about Joe, Bob, or Larry as "the father of my child," I want to know exactly what that means. Does it literally mean "the physical father of my child"? Does it mean "the man I'm still in love with"? Or does it mean "the man who constantly causes drama in my life"?

I'm not alone in this. Many men I've spoken with express the same concerns. Angelo, a twenty-four-year-old medical lab assistant, is one of them. He had plenty to say about this subject. He's experienced this on more than one occasion. Having been through relationships in the past where he's felt second to the memory of a father has made him hard. Now he makes an immediate exit when a woman starts to talk too much about the father of her child.

"They think you're supposed to accept the father because they have to. It's like you're automatically in second place. I know they have important things to talk about with the father. But too many times this man is like a third person in the relationship."

Angelo described to me his brief encounter with one woman he met while in line at a department store. He described her as a tall, slim, caramel-colored woman with hazel eyes and an energetic disposition. She'd just moved to Houston and hadn't been meeting many people, so she was open to the idea of a friendly lunch date.

"We had a nice time except she kept mentioning the name Robert [her baby's father] during lunch. She didn't mention him in a way that was romantic. She just mentioned him in the same way you would bring up the name of a good old friend. It didn't make me jealous. But I didn't see room for Robert and me too, so after lunch I didn't call her again."

Morris, a twenty-nine-year-old accountant, related a similar experience to me. He had been dating Karen for several months. He considered himself to be getting serious. Apparently Karen felt things were getting serious too. That's why she felt she had to tell him something important before they went any further. One night, she said, "Morris, I know I love you, but I'll never love anybody the way I love Jimmy [the father of her five-year-old son]."

Morris says he tried to argue that point. But he couldn't change her heart. She told Morris she loved him, but emphasized that Jimmy was the father of her child and that she could never love a man as much as she loved him.

Carl, a twenty-four-year-old insurance adjuster, says he ended a new romance with a woman named Sylvia. Not because the woman routinely talked about and saw the father of her child, but because the father would spend the night at her house when he brought the child home from his weekend visit. Needless to say, this cramped things a bit. Sylvia assured Carl that there was no hanky-panky going on. She said that it was just usually too late at night for her baby's father to make the four-hour drive home, so he would spend the night. Say what?

Just what does a woman owe the father of her child? Some

women think they have to pledge allegiance for the rest of their lives. It's as though all hopes of romance ended with him. He gets a privileged position above and beyond any other man to come in the future. In some situations, it even seems the woman is trying to hold on to the man through the baby. Grasping at memories of what is already over. In many cases, the baby seems to give her a neutral zone in which to deal with something she doesn't want to let go of. Meanwhile she completely turns off the other men who are interested in her.

On the other hand, there are women who are just attempting to provide their children with a balanced life by allowing them to be with their natural fathers. Such a woman allows the kid a good amount of quality time with the father. And sometimes this is very much for the best. For this reason, no boyfriend has the right to come into a woman's life and demand that a woman stop all communication with the father of her child. Nor should a woman allow that. Whether any of the people involved like it or not, there's an innocent child who needs both the father and the mother.

Then where does the new boyfriend fit in? Naturally he doesn't like the idea of his girlfriend being around a man she's been deeply involved with. But he has no choice other than to deal with the fact that she has certain responsibilities to her child. She has responsibilities to another man too, the baby's father. It's a tough fact that the boyfriend has to swallow.

But he has feelings that must be protected too. The woman has to realize that the new man in her life is not going to accept second place to a memory. No self-respecting man is going to sit around and listen to a woman constantly talk about another man. No self-respecting man is going to stand by while his woman has another man coming in and out of her life, or her home. She has to treat the relationship with the father in a way that doesn't compromise the child's needs, but respects her new man's feelings as well.

After solving that, there's still yet another point of view to consider: the baby's father. He has to realize that the world doesn't revolve around him. If a woman has a new man in her life, he has to respect that. To get perspective, all he has to do is look at things from the boyfriend's point of view. If that were him, he wouldn't want someone to be stepping in and out of his woman's life either. The father has a right to see his child. He should be active in the life of his child and pay child support. But he also has to realize that he has no more claim to Momma. What they had is over. He has to follow a new set of rules.

It all has to be worked out in delicate details respectful of the needs and feelings of everyone involved, especially the child. As with everything else about love and relationships, there's no easy answer. But one thing is true. This type of situation needs to be dealt with openly and honestly or there will be a big explosion down the road. This has to be discussed early on. It's not something we can just assume is understood. It can easily unravel a budding relationship. But with the right understanding, a woman, her child's father, and her new man can all get along.

SOME SUGGESTIONS TO MAKE IT WORK

Unfortunately there is no standard set of rules for this kind of situation. But there are some general guidelines women can follow to avoid more drama than is necessary.

- First and most importantly, be honest with yourself about the relationship with your child's father. Resolve any feelings you've been unable to come to terms with before bringing another man into your life. If you're still involved with the child's father, even if it's just an on-again/off-again thing, don't throw another man into the mix.

- Make sure your significant other knows the role the child's father plays in your life and your child's life. Does he call or visit often? Will this conflict with times your new man is visiting you?

- If your child's father has been extremely jealous, has stalked you, or been violent in the past, your significant other should be made aware of this. Also, men you've just started dating have a right to know this for their safety.

- Remind older children not to say awkward things that may make your significant other uncomfortable. Be prepared to smooth things over or gracefully change the subject when younger children start to talk excessively about their father.

- Don't allow arguments with your child's father to ruin the mood between you and your significant other. If this happens too often, your significant other may start to feel the situation is overwhelming him.

- Discourage any competition for the child's affection between your significant other and your child's father.

- Your significant other doesn't automatically know where he fits into the life of you and your child. Discuss this role with him.

The Good Daddies Club

Any man with the necessary physical tools can create a baby. But only a man with the right character can be a good daddy. Basically there are two types of fathers: deadbeats and daddies.

The deadbeat needs no introduction. We know him all too well from all the statistics. Some are well-educated men with high-paying careers. Some are superstar athletes. Some are blue-collar workers. Some are homeless. Many of these deadbeats have disappeared from their children's lives altogether. But some of them live right there at home with their kids. Just being in the house doesn't fulfill the obligations of being a daddy. It isn't a problem of any particular ethnic group or class, either. Deadbeats are biological fathers who don't live up to the title of daddy.

Of course, no simple formula can be applied to all fathers to determine their fitness for daddyhood. All of the factors at play aren't always apparent. There are some women who make it nearly impossible to work out a reasonable arrangement for a man to be a part-time daddy and provide full-time love for his kids. Those types of women turn children against their fathers, abuse the child-support payments, and attempt to make it difficult for men to see the children. The result is that some men whose rights have been abused and who have been pushed or barred from their children's lives may appear to be deadbeats but aren't.

Meanwhile, the good daddies go relatively unnoticed and virtually unappreciated. That's why I want to focus on some good examples. Particularly African American fathers. Too often the media makes it seem as though there are no African

American fathers except for those who are abusive or absent. So the good daddies on the other side of the scale—the loving men who are the heartbeat of their children's lives—are often forgotten. They're the good examples we don't hear about. These men not only father children, they raise them. Sometimes in the traditional nuclear-family model. Sometimes such a man can only be a daddy on his visitation days, or by paying his child support and other important costs. And some actually have custody of the kids to save them from deadbeat moms.

Unfortunately, our society tends to be obsessed with bad things. The nightly news is half an hour of bad energy. It's no different when we look at the subject of fatherhood. The problems get all the attention. Because of this, the good men are overshadowed. You won't hear much about the men who make up the membership of the Good Daddies Club on the news. Their stories and statistics aren't the subjects of studies and news specials. But know that they're out there. This essay is dedicated to them. Three of them are profiled here.

OVERTIME AND BEDTIME STORIES

Chris worked by day as an assistant manager at a grocery store. Four nights a week he also packed boxes for a local freight company. He worked hard and didn't mind it. Working hard was part of his financial planning. But his son, Brandon, was an unexpected special delivery to him and his wife after only two years of marriage. Originally they'd planned to bring a child into the world only after they'd saved enough money to purchase a home and get solidly on their feet.

Chris worked several nights, but his wife worked five nights a week as a nurse. Therefore, most of little Brandon's days and the first part of his nights were spent with his grandmother. Around 11 P.M., Chris would show up and hoist the sleepy three-year-old up on his shoulder and place him gently in his car seat. Once home, he would call his wife at work to let her know the men were home and safe.

But one night, the routine changed. As Brandon jumped into the bed, Chris clicked the light off and breathed a sigh of relief. A hot shower and cold beer would round out the night for him. He edged the door closed when he heard a tiny voice. "Daddy, can you read me a bedtime story?"

Chris lay his head against the door, wishing he hadn't heard the request. He laughed and turned the light back on. The beer would have to wait. He grabbed off the floor a copy of *The Cat in the Hat* that Brandon had been desperately trying to read. He reclined in the bed, Brandon snuggled under his arm, and he showed his son how to read the first word of the book.

PART-TIME VISITS, FULL-TIME LOVE

Jonathan takes fatherhood seriously. After a DNA test confirmed he was the father, nobody had to threaten to drag him into court. Every fifth of the month he sits down and writes out a check for 25 percent of his income and sends it to the mother of his child. Marriage was the original plan. He and Keisha were engaged and living together before their relationship fizzled out after two years of ups and downs. When they went their separate ways, they didn't know Michelle was already on the way. They even tried to revive the relationship for the sake of the child, but things still didn't come together. Despite the rift in their relationship, they made an amicable out of court settlement. He's been in compliance for five years.

Admittedly, Jonathan has some reservations about exactly where all the child-support money goes. "Sometimes I wonder if she's partying with the money. Or worse, spending it on her new man." He doesn't get an accounting of where the money goes, but he has no complaints about the baby's general appearance and happy disposition.

His fondest memory is of Michelle's fifth birthday. That morning, he packed her and four of her friends into his car. Off they went for pizza, to see *The Lion King,* and then to the park. It took him and two other parents to manage all that energy. By day's end, Michelle and her friends had thoroughly worn out the three adults. And it wasn't a cheap day either; the price of pizza, a movie, and souvenirs at the park for five-year-olds adds up fast. But the day had been worth it. He smiled as Michelle told her mother over the phone what a good time she'd had. Jonathan's story is simple and sincere. He summed it up by saying, "It would be nice to have my daughter all the time. But I'm the best daddy I can be with the time I've got."

THE DADDY WHO DOES IT ALL

Thomas knew Erica wasn't a perfect mother. She spent more time in nightclubs than she did with Gina, their ten-month-old baby. He also suspected that she wasn't taking good care of Gina. But when Erica's mother called and told him that Erica'd moved out of the state and left the baby, even he was shocked. He immediately left work, stunned. His first thought after receiving the chilling news was relief that she didn't just leave the baby on the doorstep of a stranger. But what she had done wasn't far from that. Erica had left the state to live with a man she claimed to be madly in love with. He didn't want the baby as baggage.

The first move Thomas made was to seek custody of Gina. This was something he'd wanted to do from the beginning, but he couldn't have afforded the costly custody battle that would have ensued. But now he had no problem getting custody. In fact, Erica barely escaped being prosecuted for child abandonment. After gaining custody, the real work began. He had to secure day care, which immediately snatched a large chunk of his salary as a teacher. Next, he moved to a bigger apartment and converted the second bedroom to a nursery. He was fully prepared to be a single father.

But one thing that he hadn't prepared for was the reactions of other people. Although some were proud of him, many were shocked. He says people automatically ask, "Where's the mother?"—often with an air of contempt. "People think a man can't take care of a child," he says. Then there's the dating scene. More women than you would think shy away from him because of the baby. But he doesn't let the stereotypes or lack of dates ruin his life. With all the mixing of baby formula, changing of diapers, and baby talk, Thomas wouldn't have his life any other way. He sums it all up by simply saying, "Having my daughter in my life is the best thing that ever happened to me."

Those are three good examples of fatherhood, three members of the Good Daddies Club. Not made-up but real men. Ordinary heroes who are working and doing what is right. Don't believe everything you see on television. Don't believe all the statistics you hear. There are some good daddies out there.

THINGS TO THINK ABOUT

1. What are the qualities that make a man a good daddy?

2. What can a man do to develop the qualities of a good daddy?

3. Do single fathers suffer from unfair stereotypes?

4. Would you date or marry a man who already has a child (or children)? If not, why not?

A Cure for the Tin Man

There I was, standing ready in New Orleans at the Hilton Waterfront. I was dressed in a tuxedo. My hair was in a freshly cut fade and I had a gold stud in my ear. I was one of the groomsmen in my friend Dobbin's wedding. Always a groomsman and never a groom. And I liked it that way.

After the traditional wedding ceremony we all assembled in the ballroom for the reception. We smiled for some photos, toasted the newlyweds with champagne, and cheered as they cut the cake. It was going well until the tossing of the garter was announced. All the single guys knew what this meant. As the folklore goes, the man to catch it would be the next to marry. None of us wanted to be the one.

Suddenly a curious phenomenon occurred. It was as though an alien ship were hovering above the Hilton's ballroom. A roomful of eligible bachelors suddenly froze into stiff poses, our arms became rigid, our faces took on blank stares, and we couldn't move. Not one of us headed toward the front of the ballroom. Again, another call for the single men to approach the dance floor. Realizing the threat was imminent, we took action and all started slowly creeping backward. A third call. Then I felt someone's arm hook mine and pull me through the crowd to the front. About twenty stone-faced men had been herded the same way and stood awkwardly at the front of the ballroom. We were silent, shifting our weight from foot to foot, waiting for it to be over. The only sound was the crying of a little four-year-old boy. He wanted to be a part of the toss but didn't realize he was too young.

Dobbin turned his back toward us and flung the garter over

his head. It swirled in the air. We scattered. I've never seen so many men in a room have a sudden need to check their watches. One brother folded his arms and dropped his head. Others looked away as if distracted. I stuck my hands in my pocket and pursed my lips. *Oh, God, please don't let it land near me,* I thought.

As it floated down in our direction the little boy decided he couldn't take it anymore. He broke loose from his mother and sprinted across the floor. He snatched the garter out of the air and kept running without breaking stride. With determination in his eyes, he ran away furiously. I suppose he was afraid we'd try to steal it. We all laughed. But was it funny or ironic? The only male in the room who wanted to catch the garter was a four-year-old boy.

I wonder if he will be that enthusiastic about catching the garter twenty years from now when he knows its significance. Possibly, but probably not. By that time he will have picked up the traits of the Tin Man. Like the Tin Man from *The Wizard of Oz,* he'll be a man desiring to have love in his life, yet lacking the heart necessary to experience love. He'll probably be so disconnected from his feelings that he too will glue his arms to his side, look away, and pray that the garter doesn't land by him. But how does this happen? How do men grow from the innocence of childhood into being afraid of relationships? Why do men run from love?

This legendary fear men have isn't a biological flaw. Nor does it stem from men having a screw loose in the brain. It's much simpler than that. All the problems women have with men who run from love derive from two sources: men's training and women's tolerance. The training men receive in society from the time we are boys prepares us for emotionally disconnected lives. Then, instead of insisting on an emotional connection in a relationship, many women tolerate the disconnected behavior of some men. That's how it happens. That's how ordinary little boys grow up to be heartless like the Tin Man.

We men only do what we know we can get away with. We learn what we can get away with as we grow up. We watch our mothers interact with men. Many of our impressions about male behavior come from television and movies. We watch the hero blow things up, beat people up, and enjoy a buffet of women. Those examples taught us that to be manly was to be tough and emotionally disconnected, never afraid, never giving a damn. We watched as the hero shot his way through a gunfight as his friends died around him. He never looked back. We watched as the leading man loved and left a trail of beautiful women who wanted to marry him. Ultimately the hero would always get whatever he wanted from women on his own terms.

That's where the next problem starts. Many women willingly go along with that script. They tolerate the Tin Man's behavior. They allow men to set the rules of the game. Many men then take this as a license to run wild. From their training as boys, they know what they can get away with. Men know that almost anything they pull in the love arena will be tolerated by some woman somewhere. So many women will put up with almost anything just to have a man in their lives that it creates a demand for even the most noncommittal man. It may be something she observed her mother or other women doing—chasing men or putting up with anything and everything from a man. She too is playing out a role she was trained to fill. This encourages the Tin Man to stay just as he is. He feels there's nothing wrong with him. Or, even if he feels there is something in his behavior that's wrong, he knows there's a woman somewhere who will tolerate whatever he dishes out.

Back to the ballroom floor. I may have been twenty-eight years old, but I wasn't spiritually mature. I was unprepared to engage the feelings I knew were there. I didn't know how to connect with them. It wasn't as though I could just flip a switch and be emotionally prepared to deal maturely with the ups and downs of love. Since I wasn't prepared to deal with the emotions of love, I avoided confronting my feelings for women or trying to sort them out, preferring to keep things on as light a level as possible.

Instead of seeing an intimate committed relationship as a goal, I saw it as something of a burden. Why get into a complicated love affair when I could play by my own rules? That's the way I saw it. But if I really felt that way, why was I constantly looking for a relationship? If asked, I'd say I was single and looking. And I was. I really wanted to get into a relationship. I was a member of a dating service, a singles club, and regularly consulted the classifieds looking for the right woman. Out of one side of my mouth I was saying I was looking for love. The other side of my mouth was busy speaking in code: Tinspeak, the complicated noncommittal language of the Tin Man. For the sake of women, I'm going to decipher some of that code in the hope that they will be able to recognize the Tin Man when they run across him. Fellas, do you recognize yourselves?

"I admit it. I'm just a dog"

Saying he's a dog is a cop-out. But it works because everybody buys into it. If he says he's a dog, it's as though he is excused from having to be responsible for his feelings and actions. He simply denies having any feelings. The truth is, he's out of touch with or possibly afraid of recognizing them and is using his doggish behavior as a cover.

"I'm not ready for a commitment"

This could mean a number of things. This excuse allows the Tin Man to actually cover his own fear of intimacy with seemingly good intentions. He isn't saying he doesn't want to have a relationship. He isn't saying he can't have a relationship. He's just saying he's not ready yet. But this could go on for years. Especially when you consider that he isn't trying to get ready. The truth is, he may not know how to get ready.

"I got hurt last time"

Men don't take hurt too well because they're terrified to try love in the first place. For the most part, a woman can rebound and get back into the love arena quicker than a man. After being hurt, some men sit around and brood and hold grudges for years. It's not unusual for a man to hold a new woman in his life suspect because of something another woman did. Women should use caution with men using this avoidance technique. He may in fact be very scarred by his romantic past. If he hasn't dealt with the bad feelings left over from his last relationship, you should reconsider the idea of getting involved with him.

"I'm too busy to be in a relationship"

This Tin Man excuse is hard for women to understand. But it breaks down this way: Many men see relationships as distractions and energy drains rather than power sources. Unfortunately, sometimes the wrong relationship can be not only a distraction but a setback as well. A man on the fast track in his career, in school, or attempting to establish himself may use the "I'm too busy" excuse to avoid a relationship. He doesn't want to lose himself in the ups and downs of love while he's on target to reach his goals. But hidden behind all that ambition is just plain fear. He's afraid to fall in love.

HEALING THE TIN MAN

I can spot a Tin Man within a few moments of meeting him. It takes one to know one. I'm a recovering Tin Man myself. The journey was long and hard. But I've learned how to take the leap of faith that is required in relationships. I know what it will take to cure the Tin Man because I know what cured me.

Don't fool yourself. The Tin Man isn't going to be magically cured by a woman's love. He has to cure himself. He has to decide for himself that he is tired of the fear he harbors. A friend once invited me out, and after I said I was staying home with my girlfriend, he gasped and said, "Man, I'd sure like to meet the woman who was able to get you to stop playing the field." It wasn't my girlfriend who did it, it was me. I had simply reached a point in my life where I was tired of things as they were and I decided I was going to change. When the Tin Man is ready to change, he does so of his own volition. The right woman doesn't have to push or drag him into a relationship. The only permanent changes are those he makes for himself.

However, a critical part of curing the Tin Man involves a form of positive reinforcement from women. Although they can't actually change him, women can ease his road to recovery. The following are ways women can help the Tin Man on his road to recovery:

FIVE WAYS WOMEN CAN EASE THE TIN MAN TOWARD RECOVERY

1. Don't try to steal men from other women. This only creates more opportunities for men to remain detached. When women attempt to steal married or otherwise committed men, they often try to outdo each other in terms of who can best accommodate the wishes and desires of the man. As the competition between the women increases, less and less is required of the man in the relationship. This leads to an emotionally lazy man who will have little regard for commitments or the feelings of women.

2. Don't make yourself available to a man who offers you gifts or financial assistance in exchange for time in your bedroom. Does that sound outrageous? Look around: these negotiations happen in places other than on the street corner.

3. Demand respect. What some men need is a basic lesson in human courtesy. They need to know that women have feelings and won't be there for anyone who doesn't treat them right.

4. Don't buy into the "boys will be boys" excuse. This is a cop-out that gives men license to behave badly and cheat in relationships without being held accountable for their actions. When women are willing to broad-brush the actions of men with the "boys will be boys" excuse, it sends men the signal that they can have their cake and eat it too.

5. Encourage your husband or boyfriend, father, brothers, uncles, and friends to be more than macho robots with no feelings. Encourage them to experience the full range of emo-

tions from happy to sad. If you have a son, don't raise him to be a macho robot. Don't tell your son harmful things such as "only sissies cry." Make sure he knows he can cry and play quarterback too.

THINGS TO THINK ABOUT

1. Do you feel that certain expressions of emotion are inappropriate for men? For example, is it proper for a grown man to cry?

2. What damage do you think a "macho man" mentality does to a man's feelings? What effect do you think the "macho man" mentality has on a man's physical health? His mental health?

3. Do you encourage your husband or significant other to express his feelings?

4. What can you do to encourage your husband or significant other to be more in touch with his own feelings and emotions?

LUST

Midnight Quickies

Carl gingerly rolled out of bed, trying not to disturb Lauren's sleep. But when he zipped his pants, she awakened to see him fumbling at the edge of the bed. "What are you doing?" she asked.

"Got to go, baby. I have a breakfast meeting in the morning with the regional vice president about a big new account." Carl didn't turn to look at Lauren. He squinted his face, waiting for her response. He anticipated his new lover would begin to whine, cry, and beg for him to stay.

"Okay, baby, just close the door on your way out. I'll get up and lock it in a minute." Lauren yawned and lay back down.

Carl was shocked. No whining. No dramatics. No tricks, seduction, or pleading for him to stay. For a moment, he was even a bit disappointed that she didn't seem the least bit concerned about his leaving. After he absorbed the shock, he took his time and finished dressing. *Mission accomplished,* he thought. *I hit it and quit it.*

Lauren heard the door close and listened to Carl's footsteps grow faint down the hall. She locked the door and crawled back into bed. Still nude, she lay on her back with her arms and legs outstretched. "Oooh," she said, yawning again and stretching. "That was good. But I'm glad he took his butt home." She glanced at the clock, two hours of good sleep still possible. *Mission accomplished,* she thought. *I didn't feel like being bothered with him in the morning.*

Have we replaced dating and romance with midnight quickies?

First, let's define the midnight quickie. It's a late-night or early-morning lustful intersection of two consenting adult bodies in which feelings are at a minimum and throbbing is at its maximum. It's an encounter that starts with a phone call at some hour too late for a date, but not too late for someone to stop by. This is important. Timing of this phone call is critical, because the caller doesn't want to be seen as calling to chat. The caller is on a mission. It's something detectable in the caller's tone. It's a polite but direct line of conversation. If the person called is interested, the caller will be out the door and on their way over in moments.

Obviously, the caller needs to have some sort of established relationship with the callee. This is no anonymous one-night stand with a stranger. This established relationship keeps the parties involved from feeling they are having meaningless casual sexual relations. The parties could be divorced, separated, or just friends (the elusive "F" word). But there is almost always some type of established connection.

There is only an illusion of emotion during these hot-sex "maintenance" encounters. People skilled at such calls know how to invoke passionate feelings without lies. They don't say, "I love you." Instead they will use words and phrases that bring about a facade of intimacy. A few bland "I really missed you" comments are mixed with empty flattery and light kisses on the face and neck to create an illusion of intimacy. Quickly, the two persons are all over each other in bed with legs and arms grabbing, groping, and contorting in every direction. They resemble an abstract sculpture more than a couple making love. Oh, an interruption. She has to get up to let the cat in. That's okay. It gives him time to chew the wrapper open and roll on the condom. In a few short hours, he'll be back on the road speeding home. No waking in each other's arms in this scenario. There's no time for that.

As shown, this practice isn't just a male thing. Women are aggressive players in this game too. Some turn to this practice after being burned out from too many bad relationships. Others are just out to enjoy themselves. Whatever the reason, lots of women are out there doing it too. One woman was straight with me about her habit of getting quick booty calls at midnight. She said, "You men always think women are chasing after you with a net. But I just want the same thing men want. I want a good lay to hold me over until Mr. Right comes along."

Well, isn't it easier this way? Nobody gets serious and nobody gets hurt. Besides, in today's world everyone is busy trying to make ends meet. Most of the time we're more worried about paying the car payment than falling in love. Who wants the burden of a relationship anyway? A relationship is like having an extra full-time job. You sure don't need that. You can do badly all alone, right? Besides, didn't you get crushed on the rocks of romance last time? Why expose your feelings? Having someone come over late at night to fill your physical needs is an easier arrangement. You get the *ssss-oooh* feeling for free.

So should you pick up the phone and make that call?

Before dialing the number, consider a few things. Actually, there are some dangerous realities about habitual midnight quickies. Nothing is free. Everything in life has a cost. For the opportunity of easy sexual fun, we pay the price in other areas. Foremost, there are the health risks of casual sex. The danger of contracting AIDS, herpes, gonorrhea, or a number of other sexually transmitted diseases is very real. Sleeping around is a risky practice. Gone are the days when getting a shot and taking penicillin would cure just about anything. These days not even a condom is a guarantee of safety.

Then there are the emotional costs. "Hittin' and quittin' " is bound to leave you lonely in the long run. Carl and Lauren can't go on for very long in their present arrangement. Eventually, one of two things will happen. One of them will begin to have a convenient misunderstanding about the arrangement and want to start dating and growing toward a relationship. Or they'll simply grow tired of the same old bodies and fade out of each other's lives. Either of those things may take months. Or their interest in sex with each other could wane immediately. Lauren's next three calls to Carl may end up on his answering machine, victims of the call screen. When she catches up with him, he may fade back and be distant and aloof toward her. Or, if all Lauren wants is a body, she may go to the gym and meet a man who is taller, has juicier triceps and a bigger chest than Carl.

We all have the need to be touched and loved. But the late-night quick fix isn't the right answer. At best, it's pseudo-romance. At worse, it's a cheap thrill. Yet for a moment it can fill the void and make us feel wanted, desired, and needed. That's why we're willing to play along. Perhaps that's why there's lots of sex in the world and not enough true love.

Orgasms, no matter how electrifying or scintillating, flash through the body and fade away in an instant. What's left afterward is the product of the loving that goes on outside the bedroom. But participants in midnight quickies often have only a light relationship outside the bedroom. That's why those hot encounters alone don't satisfy the hunger for love. Even people who claim to enjoy such a lifestyle eventually get tired of living that way. They begin to desire more than skin-to-skin; they crave to be soul-to-soul.

But being soul-to-soul isn't the by-product of sex. To create meaningful relationships, we must place the responsibilities of love before the fun of sex. When we fall into the habit of midnight quickies, we don't learn this important concept. Midnight quickies leave us with an unrealistic view of romance. One in which our better judgment is clouded by our passions and our sensitivity for others is dulled by quick-fix sex. It's an easy trap to fall into. But don't be blinded by lust when what you need is love.

THINGS TO THINK ABOUT

1. Sexual desires don't only occur when we are married or within a meaningful relationship. We have them all the time. What should people do when they are experiencing insatiable lust but have no intimate relationship at the time?

2. Do you believe people must have sexual "maintenance" every now and then?

3. Have you ever kept someone's number on hand exclusively for the purpose of midnight quickies?

4. Do you think habitual midnight quickies diminish our willingness to handle the challenges of establishing a full relationship?

I Thought You Were a Nice Girl!

Monique lay in bed with her mind reeling and her body tingling. With Randy, the new love in her life, lovemaking seemed to be reaching new heights. Each time they made love she felt herself drawn closer to him in the most intimate way a man and woman could be. Tonight Randy had been especially adventuresome in bed, and she loved it.

"Baby, did you like what I did to you?" Randy asked confidently.

"Mmm, yes." The words purred from Monique.

Randy laughed a little. "I know you didn't expect that. I'll bet I blew your mind, baby. There's more where that came from. You're with a man who knows how to please his woman."

Monique laughed and snuggled against Randy's shoulder. "And I know how to please my man. I've got some tricks up my sleeve that'll arch your back and make your toes curl too."

Silence.

"What do you mean by that?" Randy said, pushing Monique off of him and sitting up.

"I know how to make you happy in bed, baby. What else could that mean?"

Randy's face changed to a mask of confusion and anger. "So you're telling me you've been around? I'm in love with a freak? What other kinky things have you already done? I thought you were a nice girl!" Randy blasted.

"How dare you! What's your problem?"

"I don't want a wife who has slept with everybody in the city. That's my problem. I want to know what you've done and who you've done it with. I want names, places, positions, and all the details."

Monique ripped the blanket off the bed, grabbed her pillow, and stormed out of the room. "Randy, I'm not going to dignify you with an answer. I'm thirty-three years old. I wasn't exactly a virgin when you met me. I'll be on the sofa tonight. Good night, jerk!"

Unfortunately, Randy asked a real-life question and wanted a Girl Scout answer. But either he never should have asked that question or he should have kept a smile on his face and choked silently on Monique's answer. It's true that most men want the competitive edge in bed. We want to feel like we're blowing a woman's mind. But the hard truth is that we probably aren't. When it comes to sex, a woman, just like her man, has probably "been there and done that."

But to avoid conflict with the male ego, some women don't reveal the details of their sexual experiences. And there is the woman who won't tell a man what turns her on in bed for fear of insulting him; or worse, for fear of damaging her reputation. Instead, some women allow men to believe they're mind-blowing super-lovers, even if that isn't the case. For the sake of peace, she may moan and wiggle a little more in bed to make him feel good. Meanwhile, the man on top thinks he's in control and rocking her world. But she's really lying under him making out her grocery list. Take Tarzan and Tiffany, for example:

TARZAN (sweating): Ugh, ugh, ugh, yeah baby. You like that, don't you?

TIFFANY: Oh yeah, big daddy. Oh yeah. *[Let's see. I think I'll make a meat loaf tomorrow. I need some bell peppers, bread crumbs, tomato paste . . .]*

TARZAN (dripping with sweat): Grrr, grrr, ugh, ugh . . .

TIFFANY: Ooo, baby. Give it to me, baby. *[I think I'm out of eggs. Better pick up some bread too. I wonder when he's going to be finished. I need to do my nails tonight.]*

Randy said he'd thought Monique was a nice girl. But if he was out being a playboy for years, what does that make him? If we men have been cavorting around and sexually experimenting, isn't it logical to assume that women have too? Who would men have done it with?

The difference is that men like to boast. But women usually consider such matters personal and don't put out broadcasts of their bedroom experiences. But that sure doesn't mean they're not experienced in the bedroom. There's a simple theory of relativity behind it all. Every sexual adventure for which a man has a notch in his belt, there's a woman who has put that same notch in her garter. It's that simple.

So why are men so angry when they find out their women have had some of the same kinds of sexual escapades they've had? It's a power struggle. For most men, sex is about power. It's a matter of who's the boss, who's pleasing whom, and who's in control. A contest for power. That fear of losing control manifests itself in the fear that an experienced woman may not think a man's performance is all that much of a knockout. He's afraid that she may have had better. On the contrary, the man who feels he's in control in the bedroom feels that he has control over his woman. That's where the term "whipped" comes from. It's an insult to be called p-whipped because it means your woman's in control and not you.

Randy isn't going to keep or lose Monique in the bedroom.

However, he's on his way to losing the place of respect she has
reserved for him in her mind. Instead of being worried about
who's whipping it on whom, he should focus on other things.
First, he needs to realize that sex is just one part of a loving
relationship and not the whole purpose of the relationship.
Then he should forget about thinking of sex as a contest of
control. Last, he should learn how to please his woman. If he
really knew the secret to great sex, he would know that it isn't
just a physical thing but a meeting of minds, hearts, and souls.
Yes, Randy's lover has experience from sexual encounters in
the past. But what does that have to do with him today?

That brings us back to the problem of whether a man should
ask about a woman's sexual experience. Aside from concerns
for his health, it's really not his business to ask such questions.
If he does ask, he should be prepared: she may tell him some
stories in blunt honesty. She may even brag. It's a safe bet that
he probably won't like what she has to say. I don't think that
many men can handle too much information from a woman on
this subject. Men, you have to be realistic. Your woman probably isn't a virgin, so don't ask about her past if you can't handle
the answer. Instead, it's better to focus your energy on building
and improving your relationship. The past is the past. It's only
about whom she's with now.

THINGS TO THINK ABOUT

1. Why do you think men find it hard to accept the fact that women they are in love with have had sexual experiences similar to their own?

2. Aside from issues related to sexually transmitted diseases, do you think people should reveal details of their sexual pasts when in a relationship?

3. Are you able to express yourself sexually with your boyfriend/husband or girlfriend/wife?

4. Do you avoid discussing your sexual needs and desires with your boyfriend/husband for fear of insulting him or wounding his ego?

5. How can men and women express their sexual needs and desires to each other?

Are You Ready for a Good Man?

The consensus among men is that women don't really mean it when they say they want a good man. I have to admit that I've heard more women than I can count say the words, "I want a good man." But their actions and choices say, "I love playboys." These are the same women that later grumble, cry, and complain about how lazy and sorry their men are. Or how they had to drop a man from their lives because he was a dog. But what exactly were those women looking for in the first place?

Women who are always saying they want a good man but end up with duds need to take a long look in the mirror. Although many of them say they're sick and tired of men who cause all sorts of problems in their lives, they continue to loop back around to those same types of men time after time. This type of woman is usually sure there is nothing wrong with her. Instead, she's convinced that the men of the world are the problem. To make matters worse, she's probably surrounded by girlfriends who feel the same way, and who don't challenge her to take a look at herself and the bad choices she's making. But the problem is not as simple as blaming the man. In her book *A Return to Love,* Marianne Williamson focuses on the real issue at hand. She says, "The problem, in other words, is not that we attract a certain kind of person, but rather that we are attracted *to* a certain kind of person."* Therefore, inherent in

* Marianne Williamson, *A Return to Love* (New York: HarperCollins, 1992), p. 144.

a woman's statement "I want a good man" are the duties of self-assessment and responsibility for her own actions.

But what about passion, romance, and spine-tingling sex? I used to wonder what would make a woman get involved with a playboy, a man she knew to be a connoisseur of women. I thought playboys always lied and schemed their ways into the lives of women, and many do. But through interviewing women, I've found that many women involved with playboys know the risks of such a relationship. But they take the risk to get the benefits: passion, romance, and spine-tingling sex. The playboy isn't reliable when it comes to fidelity and honesty. But he's a specialist in generating excitement. That's what draws women to playboys: the prospect of excitement, adventure, and living on the wild side. And that's why, in so many cases, the playboy gets the initial advantage over the nice guy.

But the playboy only wins temporarily. It's the age-old race between the tortoise and the hare. Women eventually get tired of all the excitement and no follow-through. Unfortunately this is usually after learning a hard lesson. The smart women wise up and start looking for more stable and reliable men. Others, who haven't got the message, keep going back for more of the same. But why learn things the hard way? Wouldn't it be better to do a self-assessment *before* you get into another bad relationship? Be honest with yourself. Are you still a little girl seeking thrills, or are you a woman ready for love? That's the first thing you have to establish before you're ready to even seek a man. If you're a girl, don't mess up a good man with your games. If you're a woman, there's a good man out there looking for you. That's a fact. Never mind all the man-shortage statistics. When you exclude the little girls who don't know what to do with a good man, there are plenty of good men left to choose from.

LITTLE GIRLS ONLY WANT TO PLAY

We always assume that all the women who say they can't find a good man are deserving of having a good man. But just because you're a female, attractive, single, employed, and ready for a family doesn't make you a good woman. In fact, by my definition, that doesn't automatically make you a real woman at all. Before we go any further, we have to separate the little girls from the women.

What I consider a little girl has nothing to do with age. A little girl is any grown woman too emotionally young to realize that life isn't a big birthday party thrown for her. Little girls want to play. That's why they love playboys. They get excited easily and act upon that excitement with reckless abandon. Little girls don't think about tomorrow. They just let their passions run wild and don't worry about the consequences. They're easy prey for men with sexy bodies. They shamelessly chase men who have money. They reward well-dressed smooth talkers with their phone numbers. For them, all that matters is what they can see and touch.

That's why a little girl has no place in a relationship with a good man. If she gets her hands on one, she'll run him into the ground. She doesn't know what to do with a good man. She's not a good woman yet.

WOMEN ARE FOR REAL

On the other hand, a woman has graduated from girlhood. She knows from life's experience that having one good man is better than being out all the time playing with boys. While she appreciates fine bodies, financially successful men, and excitement in a relationship, she can't be easily swept away by those things because she is planted in reality. This woman doesn't need a man to come into her life to make her feel like she's alive. She's developed her own passion for life. It's evident in her personality, her career, and her glowing aura. She's vibrantly alive with or without a man in her life. When she's in a relationship, it's about sharing. She seeks to exchange good vibrations with a man who can return the same energy.

Ultimately, we choose whom we become involved with. The date and time we meet them may seem to occur by chance, but establishing a connection by giving someone your phone number or setting up a date removes the element of chance from things. It adds the certainty that you are interested or at the very least curious to know more. Granted, you can't know much about someone at first, but it won't take long for red flags to start popping up along the way if they aren't right for you. Whether you choose to heed those warnings is another matter altogether.

Valerie Shaw, author of *Himpressions,* spoke this as gospel to women: "You definitely attract what you want by affirming it in thought, word, and action." Shaw asks women to take a simple quiz to determine if they are dogcatchers:

ARE YOU A DOGCATCHER?

1. Are you into thrills (this does not necessarily mean adventure)?
2. Are you bored if he doesn't have a good line?
3. Does your first date or first kiss have to crinkle your toes and turn your brain to mush?
4. Would you rather have his money than his time?
5. Does his car, house, dog, or job overly impress you?
6. Are you into power (with a capital P)?
7. Does his style hold more of your attention than his smile?

8. Does it bother you if he stutters, stammers, or is clumsy when he tells you how much he cares for you?

9. Does getting laid mean more to you than being loved?

10. Would you rather have his gold than share his goals?*

Shaw says a "yes" to any of the above questions means a woman is a possible dogcatcher.

If you're working as a dogcatcher, that explains why you keep catching dogs. You don't go to the dog pound to find a good man. If you keep getting involved with jerks, something is wrong. But look inside yourself for the answer first. Remember the old adage, "Fool me once, shame on you. Fool me twice, shame on me." If you want a good man in your life, stop and ask yourself some honest questions about what you think is important in a man. Then refer back to Shaw's quiz and change your life where necessary. It all comes down to one simple fact: you won't find a good man if you're not ready.

* Valerie Shaw, *Himpressions* (New York: HarperCollins, 1996), p. 52.

THINGS TO THINK ABOUT

1. Men often complain that women say they want a good man but then get involved with playboys. Does this statement ring true for you?

2. Is the excitement of a playboy just a growth phase for most women?

3. Are "nice guys" boring?

4. How can couples balance their desire for excitement with needs for stability in a relationship?

Her Cheating Heart

We've heard all about the cheating men out there. They're the subjects of books, movies, television shows, statistics, and psychological studies. Observing all the furor over male cheating, one would think that only men are capable of such behavior. It almost makes it sound as though we are the only ones who lie about working overtime, meeting a friend for dinner, or going away on a business trip. But that isn't the whole story.

There's a flip side to cheating. Just as men have been free to do whatever they wanted in the past, women are equally empowered today. Women cheat too and they're doing it in increasing numbers. That's why we'll never get past the betrayal of cheating without acknowledging both sides of the coin. Cheating isn't a gender problem. It's a human problem that all of us are susceptible to.

But even though both genders do it, men are seen as less than human if they fall from monogamous grace. When men cheat, they're called "dogs." However cheating women often get a different treatment. When women cheat, they're more likely to get the benefit of the doubt as to why they cheated. Instead of looking at the woman's error, we search for a reason to understand why she cheated. "What did he do to cause this?" is often the question—that is, how did her man drive her to do this? It almost always leads back to the fault of a man, usually her husband or a past boyfriend. Once the man becomes the source of the problem, the woman is relieved of the responsibility for her actions.

But let's be honest and realistic. Men aren't really the only cause of women cheating. Women are human and therefore just as capable of cheating as men. They have the choice of whether or not to cheat. I interviewed female cheaters who've talked about, even bragged about their exploits. Though some did cite emotional neglect or cheating by their men as their excuse for cheating, not all of them did. Some of the female cheaters said they did it because they were bored in their relationships. Others said they were looking for sexual thrills. From those women, I learned the six reasons and justifications women use for cheating: (1) The Equalizer, (2) The Mind Trick, (3) The Dupe, (4) The Arrangement, (5) The Player, (6) Something Just Happened.

THE EQUALIZER

"Men do it." This is the battle cry for the equalizer. Some women I interviewed believe cheating is their way of keeping equal ground in a relationship with men who cheat. These women think they are somehow going to prevent themselves from being hurt in a relationship by cheating on a cheating man. Some "equalizers" even make an effort to keep pace with their cheating men. The more she thinks he's cheating, the more she cheats. It's a type of "an eye for an eye" justice that goes around in circles.

THE MIND TRICK

The mind trick is used to make the man feel that something he did wrong makes a woman go out and cheat. For example, she may say that he doesn't give her enough attention, or isn't romantic enough. The logic is that if he had never done something wrong, she wouldn't have had to go out and cheat. On the surface it sounds sensible. But underneath there's no logic to it. It may get her off the hook. But what's left is two people living a lie.

THE DUPE

This is a method often used by a woman who is bored in her current situation. She pretends everything is perfect. She's always sweet and nobody would ever suspect she was fooling around. She'd never do anything like that, right? Wrong! This is a passive strategy used to maintain a happy-couple image while she gets whatever else she wants on the side. But that illusion can't last forever. Situations such as the dupe have a way of unraveling themselves. No matter how careful a woman is when "duping" a man, she will eventually leave some evidence of her extramarital activities. Perhaps she'll get an unplanned phone call while her husband is home. Maybe her husband will discover a note from her lover that she carelessly left around the house. Or maybe she'll even be spotted with her lover somewhere by a friend of her husband. It happens all the time.

THE ARRANGEMENT

"You live your life and I'll live mine." This is a mutual agreement between a cheating husband and a cheating wife. Together they have a home, cars, and kids. But little or no interest in each other. Rather than lose it all, they stay together and lead separate lives. Less than a marriage or committed relationship, it is simply an arrangement. They conduct themselves as a couple on the surface, but live very separate love lives. Both she and her spouse have a mutual agreement not to ask each other questions about their private lives.

THE PLAYER

This woman has one man who holds the official title of boyfriend or husband. Meanwhile she maintains as many men as she can on the side. She wants them to be available for whatever she needs from them. Some of the men in her collection are for conversation and light dating, some are for money, and some for sex. Like her male player counterpart, she tries to keep all of her playthings under control. Always on the take, everybody and everything in her life is for her pleasure. She's a heartbreaker who will tell a man whatever he wants to hear to get what she wants.

SOMETHING JUST HAPPENED

This is my favorite. To avoid admitting responsibility for cheating, too many women fall back on the old "something just happened" theory. That just doesn't fly. Let me get this right. She just happened to be in a dark and cozy jazz bar while her husband was out of town. Then she just happened to have some wine with a handsome man she had been flirting with over the phone for weeks. They just happened to go to his house. There, they just happened to start kissing and squeezing each other. Then they just happened to go upstairs to the bedroom. Then they just happened to get undressed. Magically, he just happened to be in bed with her and then . . . something just happened?

It's obvious that, to do all that, a woman has to be well aware of what is going on. Which is the point. Guys, don't mislead yourself about the truth. At worst, she planned this scenario. At best, she put herself into a compromising situation and didn't walk away when things got too hot. Either way, it didn't just happen. She knowingly passed the threshold of acceptable behavior.

DO YOU KNOW YOUR LBT?

Both men and women have what I call a "lust bust threshold." You know what I'm talking about. That nine point nine on a scale of ten. The one moment you know lust has taken full control of your mind and body. For women it may be a touch on the small of the back, a deep voice, or a hard body. For men it might be long sleek legs, a touch on the chest, or a soothing feminine voice. Whatever it is, we all have something that can push us right to the line. Nothing "just happens." We have the responsibility to turn away when we feel things could get out of control.

Some people have very high, seemingly unshakable LBTs. An example of someone with a high-tolerance LBT is a person who can say, "I'm not interested. I'm committed to my relationship"—despite a proposition from an attractive and charming man or woman. But a person with a low LBT would dive right into bed and forget the names of their spouse, kids, and dog faster than they could take off their clothes. Whatever your LBT is, you need to become familiar with it. Take inventory of what fuels your sexual appetite well in advance of a tempting situation. That way you can spot trouble and avoid it before it starts to work its way into your mind.

Here's the bottom line on cheating: When you strip away all the excuses, revenge-based justifications, and greedy motives, cheating very simply breaks a promise. Not simply a promise made to be faithful to another person, but a promise we made to ourselves. Even if the cheating is never discovered, a bond has been broken and the relationship is drastically altered. Above all else, remember the golden rule: "Do unto others as you would have others do unto you."

This goes for both men and women. As I mentioned earlier,

cheating doesn't know any gender, color, age, or religious lines. It's here on earth tempting us all. And we're only human. We don't always make it through the temptations. That's when we make up excuses. We have developed a thousand convenient what-ifs to answer the charge of cheating. But cheating is cheating. When it's time to start cheating that is a signal that we need to turn inward to ourselves and our significant other to find out what needs to be done to repair things. A desire to cheat tells us that it's probably time to step back and reassess the relationship. It may be time to move on, because sneaking out the back door and hiding our tracks with lies is a terrible mistake for everyone concerned.

Despite what some boyfriends or husbands may be lacking in the area of excitement, emotional sensitivity, financial security, or bedroom talent, women cheating is not the answer to solving any problems. Just as there's no excuse for any man to cheat, neither is there an excuse for any woman to cheat. I'm not trying to be holier than thou. I'm talking from my own experience from both sides of the line. As the cheater and the cheated upon. It just isn't worth it. I don't ever want to invite that kind of confusion back into my life. It's better to exercise self-control, practice the golden rule, and above all don't put yourself into compromising situations.

THINGS TO THINK ABOUT

1. Some women say their husbands or boyfriends drove them to cheat. How else could they have addressed the problems that caused them to cheat?

2. Why do some people cheat instead of ending their relationship?

3. Do you believe that saying "something just happened" is an excuse for cheating?

4. Do you have a high or low LBT (lust bust threshold)?

Shoes Don't Make the Man

"You can tell everything about a man by his shoes."

I've heard too many women quote that phrase as if it were a fact etched in stone. But it's not that simple. Little sayings like that don't always tell the whole story. I agree that to an extent clothing can be representative of a person and can be used to send deliberate nonverbal communications. Through clothing we can broadcast controlled messages to the world about who we are and what we want to be without uttering a single word.

But clothing can't be the only basis for analyzing a person's character. In a world where you can buy anything on credit, clothes are less a representation of who a person is and more a representation of how a person desires to be perceived. Add the combination of television and large department stores and anyone can mimic styles from coast to coast. That's why a kid in Omaha, Nebraska, can walk into Sears wearing Levi's and a T-shirt and walk out looking like Snoop Doggy Dogg.

But yet we still have women who rely on old sayings about men being worth as much as their shoes. Far too many women still think that the character of a man is shown through his clothing. The problem with this assumption is that women are duping themselves. There are plenty of men who barely have money in the bank who look like millionaires every day of the week. They invest in their clothing. The key word being "invest." These men know that fine clothes and some smooth talking can go a long way with women who believe that "clothes make the man." By looking and talking the part men get the attention of women who have jobs, cars, and homes, unlike themselves. Next thing you know, the men are borrowing money, lying around at the woman's house, driving her car, and using her gas (sometimes to see other women). All that from one shiny pair of Italian shoes.

Nightclubs are the best place to observe this kind of illogic. Most of the women are gravitating toward the best-dressed men. But everybody is a star on Saturday night. Nightclubs are full of men who are faking an image. The man in the Giorgio Armani may not even have a job. The brother sporting the Hilfiger may have borrowed tonight's cover charge from his buddy. The man profiling against the wall in his Perry Ellis may have just skipped parole. I wish I were joking. But those men have a better chance of getting the attention of the ladies than a neat but plainly dressed man in "no name"-brand shoes and a suit from the two-for-one sale at a men's discount clothing store. Ironically, the plainly dressed man may have three times the financial stability of the well-dressed fakers.

But the illusions work like a charm. I've seen fakers work their magic right into a woman's bed, heart, and pocketbook. I know of one man who used to fake a more complete business image than most of the real businessmen I knew. One Friday evening I was hurrying down the aisles of a grocery store grabbing things and tossing them into my basket. As I rounded the corner and got to the milk, I ran into him. There he stood in his investment. This brother was sharp. He was posing in a three-button wool-and-mohair suit by Nino Danieli, silk tie by Pavone, cotton shirt by Mondo di Marco, and even the O.J. trial didn't stop him from wearing his beloved Bruno Magli shoes. In about two thousand dollars of clothing he looked more like an investment banker than the con man he was.

His act didn't stop there. Mr. Con even had fake business cards, a phony business listing in the White Pages, and a real answering service for his fake business. The icing on the cake was his charm. That's what made his front work so well. He could sell you the Brooklyn Bridge. His smoothness earned him the pick of many eligible bachelorettes, as well as married women, around the city. He often boasted about how much money he borrowed from women. He told story after story of his sexual exploits. He even bragged about stealing from the homes of his lovers when he had the opportunity. But it all finally caved in on him when he was caught using some credit cards he'd stolen. He's in jail now.

I'm sure some of his victims could get a spot on the Ricki Lake show with their stories of how this no good man tricked them and then used them for sex, money, and a place to stay. But before the eyes start rolling and the necks start jerking, those women need to check themselves. If they were so drawn to his shoes, suit, and car, what were they looking for in the first place? Were they looking for love or what they thought they could get from him? It takes two to tango. It's hardly ever just the man who is on the take.

Of course, a woman wants to be with a man who has good grooming habits and proper attire. No woman would want to show up at an important business function with a man who's not appropriately dressed. No woman wants to go to dinner with a man whose clothes look as though they badly need ironing. And women don't like to date men with dingy scuffed-up shoes. That's quite understandable. But this isn't about tacky dressing or slobs. It's about making a vast overassumption. Believing that the clothing means success. Or shoes mean stability. A nicely dressed handsome man is just that. No more, no less. Until you know more, it's safest to admire only that much about him. If he also turns out to be the man of your dreams, that's fine. But don't assume he is. Shoes don't make the man.

THINGS TO THINK ABOUT

1. There's nothing wrong with admiring a well-dressed man, but do you make assumptions about a man's character based on the clothes he's wearing?

2. Have you ever made assumptions about a man from the clothes he was wearing and then found those assumptions to be wrong? How were your assumptions wrong? Was it a pleasant surprise or did you feel as though you'd been tricked?

3. In a social setting, such as a party, do you overlook the men who are plainly dressed?

The "F" Word

Earnest rolled his Oldsmobile slowly along the row of restaurant windows facing the parking lot. Inside he could see the lunch crowd. Hundreds of corporate types bunched around tables trying to stretch fun, food, and a bit of relaxation into an hour. Earnest's eyes bounced on and off each person who didn't match what he was looking for. Coming to the last window at the back of the restaurant, he sighed. He started laughing at himself for thinking he'd overheard his wife, Donna, setting up a secret lunch rendezvous. His heart rate returned to normal.

But as he started to turn the wheels of his car away, he casually glanced back for the last time. Then it hit him. His eyes were drawn to a cocoa-colored woman with loose braids neatly drawn back into a ponytail. It was Donna. And she was throwing her head back in laughter. And yes, she was with a man. A good-looking man who was laughing harder than she was. She was fooling around. He did hear what he had thought he heard her saying on the phone last night? When he was stepping out of the shower, she was planning a secret rendezvous with her lover. Were they laughing at him? Yeah, they were laughing at him for being such a fool, he thought.

His temper flared. He slammed the car into park and jumped out. Earnest stormed through the doors of the restaurant and marched past the hostess, who asked him if he needed a table. In his march of madness he stepped on a woman's foot, bumped a seated man in the head, offering no apology, and almost knocked a waiter with a tray full of sizzling fajitas to the floor.

Arriving at their table at the back of the restaurant, his face curled from the heat of his anger. His voice was a growl. Everything went into slow motion. "What the hell is going on here?" he demanded of his wife.

She was shocked to see him. "Earnie. Is something wrong, honey?"

"What the hell is going on here?" he blasted again.

She frowned in confusion. "Nothing, we're just having lunch and cracking jokes about that bubbleheaded boss of ours. You remember my co-workers from the Christmas party, don't you?" She pointed at each one as she spoke. "Don, Marie, Lydia, and George."

"Are you sure you're feeling well, guy?" said Don.

Earnest's narrowly focused eyes drew back to a wide angle. He saw that she wasn't sitting at the table alone with a man. She was with four people at a large table in the back of the restaurant. All eyes were focused on him as he tried to back away with as much of a humble grin as he could muster.

He had lots of explaining to do that night.

But was he completely crazy? What if Donna were looking out the window of their happy home and saw a woman in a black 300ZX whiz up to drop Earnest off after work? What if all she could see behind the darkly tinted windows was a smooth young face, succulent red lipstick, and a head of long thick hair that shook as she eagerly waved goodbye to a grinning Earnest. Would the first thing that popped into her mind be "Oh that must be the nice girl in the accounting department Earnie is always talking about"? I doubt it. The first instinct would be defensive. "Who's this little hoochie trying to steal my man?"

Earnest and Donna's scenario may seem extreme. But we all have some of them in us. I can see myself jumping to the same

conclusion that Earnest did. And I've been on the receiving end
of women jumping to conclusions as well. We all have some
legitimate concerns about what our significant others mean
when the word "friend" is applied to a person of the opposite
sex. For some reason the word is often twisted, bent, and
misused. Mostly on purpose. I always think it's best to clarify
the notorious "F" word before it becomes an issue.

Many of us have one-track thinking when a friend of the
opposite sex is mentioned, especially men. We automatically
think the word "friend" means a potential threat—someone
our woman used to screw, wants to screw, or is planning to
screw. And women are guilty of that thinking too. But again,
that's because so many people intentionally twist the "F" word
into a hiding place for their true intentions. People who twist
the meaning of the "F" word use friendship as a cover for
telephone conversations, meetings, lunches, and dinners that
really aren't only friendly in nature. It's usually much later that
their significant other finds out that the "friend" wasn't only a
friend, but a lover in a clandestine affair. But not everyone is
like that. The reality is that many men and women do have true
friends of the opposite sex. If that "friend" is really just a
friend, they pose no threat to your relationship or marriage.

We all know that men and women can have more than just
sexual desire between them. Truly platonic friendships aren't
controlled by sexual energy. Contrary to popular belief, men
and women can maintain relationships that aren't always flirting
with the bedroom if the people involved are spiritually mature
enough to handle the situation. When we're in a relationship or
married, we don't have to cut ourselves off from the world by
avoiding contact with the opposite sex. We just have to follow
some simple guidelines to keep friendships friendly and within
the bounds of good taste.

Webster's dictionary defines "platonic" as "not sexual but purely spiritual." Having platonic friendships while in a relationship or married requires three things: (1) mature attitudes, (2) trust, and (3) respect. This is an area in which a relationship needs some concrete rules. By sticking to these rules, some big arguments, and even a breakup, can be avoided.

And please note, having rules about friends of the opposite sex isn't about losing your freedom and having to report to someone else. This is about mutual respect. If you're in a relationship and you feel as though the following rules are about reporting in to somebody, you need to take a look at your relationship. If you care for and respect someone, telling them where you're going and what you're doing is more about sharing than reporting.

PLATONIC RELATIONSHIP RULES

1. Don't forget that a friend can't take the place of your significant other. The friend comes second. Your relationship is first.
2. Let your significant other know who your friends are. Be honest about how your friendship started and the history of your friendship with that person. Introduce your significant other to your friends.
3. Never flirt with disaster by disguising an affair of the heart as a friendship.
4. Drop friends whose behavior doesn't respect your boundaries. Such behavior would include sexual innuendos, inappropriate humor, and lack of respect for your significant other.
5. Pull back from friendships if you feel yourself slipping into more.
6. Don't divulge intimate secrets of your love relation-

ship to any friends, male or female. Intimate details are private matters to be shared between you and your significant other.

7. Don't seek comfort in a friend of the opposite sex instead of your significant other. If you have something you can't discuss with your lover, go to a trusted friend of the same sex or to a pastor or counselor.

8. Don't maintain close friendships with people whom your significant other has a legitimate reason for being uncomfortable with.

9. Don't constantly talk about the friend as though he/she is a third person in your relationship.

10. Don't meet friends without disclosing this to your significant other. This avoids unnecessary confusion.

And remember, if you have any doubts about what's appropriate behavior, recall the golden rule: Don't do anything you wouldn't want your significant other to do. It's that simple. A good relationship is a blessing too good to let slip away for a fleeting moment of lust. Undefined friendships with the opposite sex can sometimes get out of control. But with a little planning, the "F" word doesn't have to be a bad word.

Color-Struck

"I like my women light, bright, and damn near white."

I wouldn't have believed that statement if I hadn't heard it with my own ears. Here we are at the end of the twentieth century. A time in which we've gone from horse and buggy to space shuttles. From telegraphs to cellular phones. From structures of brick and wood to skyscrapers of steel and glass. Yet at the close of this dynamic century, one thing still hasn't changed: black folks are still color-struck.

I grew up on the heels of the Black Power movement. But despite all the Afros, cornrows, and people singing, "Say it loud, I'm black and I'm proud," I vividly remember blacks of that time still being color-struck. It was as though the idea that "black is beautiful" had never been born. As black kids, we were still learning misperceptions of black beauty from many of the black adults around us. Where they left off, the media picked up and finished the lesson. We quickly felt the reality of the old saying "White is all right, brown can stick around, and black better stay back." Among ourselves, we preserved the color phobia as well. I still haven't forgotten a version of tag we played called "Black African." For us, running from the tag of the Black African was serious business. If caught, you were the Black African for the rest of the day, and everyone would avoid you.

The messages about blackness we received from the non-black majority culture around us were generally negative. Since we were kids, we didn't know what was wrong with being black, we just accepted that it was bad. It was bad on television. The people in Tarzan movies were ignorant, black, half naked, and running around with spears screaming in the jungle. They were so black that on a black-and-white television they were just inky patches when they weren't smiling. In grade school, one of my teachers spoke of the wild and evil civilizations of deepest, darkest Africa. Such were the cues we were getting. It wasn't good to be black. We were learning to associate being dark with ignorance, savagery, and, above all, ugliness.

But the negative messages came from inside the black community as well. The color phobia of our race further extends itself into an ignorant, self-loathing social system with the darkest of the dark at the bottom and the most white in appearance at the top. Many blacks would like to pretend that this mentality died out decades ago, but it didn't. I grew up hearing black people use dark skin as the punch line of jokes and as a put-down. When I was a kid, the way to really insult someone was to call them a "black nappy-headed" something-or-other. I even remember hearing the high-yellow colored parents of a friend referring to other African Americans as "Black Sambos" and "blue-black niggers." Although that thinking was totally backward, it was the prevalent tone of society, and was burned into our minds.

Our bodies may be free, but our minds are still shackled as long as we hold on to the ignorance of being color-struck. Many of us claim to be full of black pride and Afrocentric. We display African artwork on our walls. We proudly accent our clothing with Kente neckties, purses, and handkerchiefs. We purchase memberships in the NAACP and buy tickets to the banquet every year. Some of us can even sing two verses of "Lift Every Voice and Sing" before we start lip-synching. But for many blacks this is more smoke screen than truth. Many of the same black folks who call themselves champions of the cause are the very folks who brag about their "good hair" and creamy light skin. As long as we think that way, we are still enslaved.

Certainly, I'm not saying that a person who has light skin and wavy hair is any less black than a person with dark skin. The fact of the matter is that almost all Americans are mixed with the blood of more than one ethnicity. I don't have to go far on either side of my family tree to find several Native Americans and some Irish ancestry. But light-skinned blacks are just that—black. The same goes for dark-skinned blacks. The dangerous thing is that we continue to think of ourselves not as African Americans but as dark-skinned blacks and light-skinned blacks. We practice a level of prejudice within our own race that would have us marching in the streets if any other group dared to do it.

One place that practice can be observed is in the meaning of the old southern slang term "pretty girl." A "pretty girl" is a woman with light skin and long straight or curly "good" hair. She may be that way from genetic chance or selective breeding, or she may be biracial. No matter how she got that way, she'll bear the mixed blessing of being considered pretty simply because of her likeness to whiteness.

This is nothing but plantation mentality. But there are more than a few men who think that way. Too many black men rank beauty on how close a woman is to looking white. They have a backward mentality in regard to beauty, which they rank as follows:

1. Throughout black history, the half-white biracial bombshell has automatically been the queen of black beauty— simply because she's half white. A fact that is inherently

contradictory and reveals some troubling things about the mentality of some blacks.

2. In second place is any biracial bombshell of any mixed blood. She can claim beauty-queen rights as long as she is half anything other than black.

3. Third place would go to any woman with light skin. She too can enjoy the benefits of being a beauty queen, as long as she has the coveted features of fair skin, a small nose, thin lips, sparkling brown or green eyes, and "good hair."

4. For men who live by this absurd twisted concept of beauty, the woman with dark skin comes after all the others. Why? Simply because she has dark skin.

The reader should note here that I'm not suggesting that biracial, dark-skinned, light-skinned, or nonblack women aren't inherently attractive. Beauty is beauty, no matter what package it comes in. Black Americans need to realize that black is already beautiful in whatever form it is in. Standards of black beauty don't have to mimic the appearance of people who don't look like us. But a troubling mentality still exists among those black Americans who don't realize that their features are beautiful too.

Aggravating the situation, feeding this ignorance, are black men who exclusively seek out the lightest, brightest woman they can find. She doesn't need an education, money, or talent; the light skin can be her ticket to his heart and bank account. Ironically, many of these brothers wouldn't be caught holding hands with a white woman. But they want a black woman who looks white. They fall to their knees every night begging God for a Vanessa Williams, Halle Berry, or Jasmine Guy to walk into their lives.

I can easily understand why darker-toned women sometimes get on the defensive about their looks. In our society, beauty is defined largely by likeness to whiteness. Therefore, many blacks have a standard of beauty that doesn't even match their own features. It's no small wonder that we find many black women who desire to have attributes that aren't natural to them. Some black women try to change their eyes, hair, bodies, and even their actual skin color to be acceptable by a standard of beauty that is not designed for them.

I remember the words of a woman I once dated. After much primping in the mirror, she finally said with confidence, "I think I'm pretty for a dark girl." I cringed, but understood her painful statement. She meant that in spite of her dark skin, she still managed to correct her looks to make herself somewhat pretty. The same happens with the idea of "good hair." To call some hair good and other hair bad means that there is a standard in relation to something. If "good hair" is long and wavy, then bad hair must be short and curly.

Women attempt to compensate for "bad hair" by making it "good." This is done by frying it with red-hot combs, bathing it in lye, or subjecting it to the infamous perm until it submits in straightness and becomes "good hair." Lately we've had the same issue with eye color. Does every woman who wants to be beautiful have to stick green, light brown, and even ice-blue contacts into her eyes? Fashion and style are one thing, but shame and self-hatred are another. We're so deep into the confusion that we don't even know where one starts or ends anymore.

Dark women, you are beautiful. There's nothing wrong with your skin or features. The politics of skin color is an infection in the minds of black America. It is ignorance and self-hatred disguised so well that we can't see it. Remember, "black is beautiful.'' Dark skin is powerful, alluring, and mysterious. Don't allow the ignorance of others to define your beauty.

Light-skinned women, you are beautiful. You've endured the arrows from both sides of the battle. On one side, you're besieged by those who hail you as queens of black beauty simply because of your skin. On the other side, you are despised by some people with darker skin and accused of thinking you're better than everyone else. But your skin and features are just as black and just as beautiful. Don't allow the ignorance of others to define your beauty.

Furthermore, this goes for black women of all the shades in between. All of you have beautiful skin. Looking at the flavors of black women is like being in an ice cream store. There is Mocha, Amaretto, Dutch Chocolate, Butter Pecan, and Caramel, to name just a few. All of those flavors are tasty. The light skin is just as beautiful as dark skin. Ultimately, like the old adage says, beauty is only skin deep. Skin, be it dark or light, is only a covering. The focus of beauty should be the woman inside. True beauty is something that radiates from the interior of the soul, not from the surface of the skin.

THINGS TO THINK ABOUT

1. Romantically, do you prefer men or women with a particular skin color? Why?

2. Have you ever experienced conflicts with other African Americans based on skin color?

3. Were you taught any prejudices against other African Americans based on skin color?

4. Is the issue of being color-struck getting any better?

5. How can African Americans who are color-struck move beyond that mind-set?

Who Should Pay?

We followed the waiter through the crowded restaurant out onto the patio. I pulled out a chair for my date, and she sat down at our table for two with a view of the bay. We dined on fresh grilled seafood in the gentle ocean breeze as the sun set over the water. For dessert, we swapped funny stories from childhood over cheesecake and strawberries. After dinner, the waiter approached with a smile and placed the check before me. "I'll take care of this when you're ready, sir." Like a programmed robot, I reached for it. But before I could get my hand on it, my date took the check.

I suppose that deeply ingrained traditions cause a waiter to do such things. It's also those same old traditions that caused me to automatically reach for the check. But that's just one of many outdated customs that linger in our society today without good reasoning to support them. Some old traditions just don't apply anymore. These days it's not a foregone conclusion that the man is paying. It just so happens that on this particular evening I wasn't paying for dinner. In fact, my date had a salary that was easily twice my income. She'd asked me to go to dinner with her and intended to pay from the very beginning.

But I haven't dated many women like that. Usually an interesting silence falls over the table when the check arrives. The liberated, independent, outspoken, and opinionated woman I came into the restaurant with gets quiet. Really quiet. Suddenly it's the old days, and I'm supposed to pay the check just because I'm the man. I think that's nonsense.

I don't object to paying for the entire date sometimes. But I don't want to feel as though I am supposed to pay just because I'm a man. It's not a question of being a gentleman either. Chivalry isn't dead. I will, as a matter of habit, open doors for a woman, pull out her chair at the table, stand to offer my seat, and pick up something a woman drops. I was raised that way. Although I have encountered women who were offended by such things, most women I know feel it's appropriate if done with proper intentions.

But who should pay the check isn't a question of chivalry. Being a gentleman has absolutely nothing to do with paying the check at dinner. It has nothing to do with who should pay for the movie. Being a gentleman doesn't mean that the man should pay for everything all of the time. It's no more a man's responsibility to pay all the time than it is a woman's job to stay home barefoot and pregnant. Thank God, we just don't live in those times anymore.

By automatically placing the check on the man's side of the table, that waiter was putting all the financial burden on the man. Isn't that reverse sexism? This isn't the 1950s. Back then the common practice of society was for the man to pay for everything on a date, because he automatically made more money and had infinitely more privileges than the woman. Take marriages of those days as an example. The man was, in most cases, the sole commander of the family. He owned everything: the house, the car, the wife, the kids, and the dog. His wife probably didn't work outside the home. That left her without an income and totally dependent on her husband. Obviously, in that case, the man had to pay for everything. But most people don't live that way today, and the idea that the man should always pay for the date is obsolete.

However, there has sometimes been an exception where blacks are concerned. Traditionally, the black man hasn't automatically been the sole breadwinner. When I was growing up, both of my parents worked hard, and that's how the parents of most of my friends were. Which is precisely my point. Many black men aren't able to wine and dine a woman and pay for everything all the time. But that's not just a black-man thing. It's a man thing, period. For all Americans, middle-class living is supported by dual incomes. So how can dating traditions be based on one male income?

As with many of our problems today, this one is rooted in modern people trying to live by the traditions of a bygone era. Cinderella couldn't get a date in today's romantic market because she'd be sitting around the house waiting for Prince Charming to come along and do everything for her. That old Cinderella thinking won't work in today's rapid-paced world where money is tight and stress is high. Today, the belief that a man is supposed to come into a woman's life and take care of her is ludicrous. Most American families couldn't sustain their standard of living without two incomes. Especially where black men and women are concerned. Look at black history. Then look around in your circle of friends. Not many of them could support an entire family on one income. When you get down to it, we're all just trying to make it out here. So again I ask, how can the man be expected to pay for everything?

More outrageous and even insulting is that some women think men are supposed to pay for everything because she's in possession of something between her legs that a man will do anything to get. This type of woman believes that if a man wants to spend any time with her, he has to pay for it through gifts, dinners, vacations, ''loaning'' her money, etc. Sadly enough, many men and women are happy to play that game of sexual quid pro quo.

But women enjoy good sex as much as men do. Experienced men know that. They know there are ready, willing, and able bodies out there somewhere that want sex as much as they do. A man doesn't have to spend money on a woman to get sex. If a man is in the habit of using money and gifts to get sex, it's probably for his own ego reasons. Or he just doesn't know what's up in the world around him. Sex is a two-way street. It's not as though the man doesn't have anything to offer a woman during sex. He's contributing his body and at least half the effort. If things work out well enough, both will have a good orgasm. So why should he have to pay?

It all comes back around to being fair in a relationship. The thinking behind splitting the check promotes fairness. There's a big difference in "Let me pay the check" and "You should pay the check because you're a man." Nobody wants to be in a relationship in which they feel they're being used or taken advantage of. A man doesn't want to feel that he's being used as a meal ticket. Likewise, a woman doesn't want to feel that she's being wined and dined because a man wants to get her into bed. When things are on equal ground, both the man and woman feel better about the whole relationship. For those couples where down-the-middle splitting isn't possible, things should at least be divided up along the lines of what each can afford to contribute. And this shouldn't stop at dinner. It should expand to all of the financial and emotional activities in a way that is fair to both sides. This includes splitting the responsibility to talk, listen, and be nurturing when necessary. Each person should be contributing something. It's simply a matter of fairness.

Of course, all of this doesn't mean that someone can't treat you to a night out. It just means that they don't have to. On my date, I was being treated. When the waiter came back, my date handed him the check and her credit card. "Just add your tip," she told him. We walked out laughing about the whole thing. Of course, being a gentleman, I held the door open for her as we made our exit.

THINGS TO THING ABOUT

1. Would you object to paying for a date? Sharing expenses on a date?

2. Is the saying "No romance without finance" part of your personal philosophy? Why?

3. Should the man pay most of the expenses within a marriage? Why?

Sexy Legs and Herpes Too

I'm not going to shake a self-righteous finger at anyone with herpes or any other sexually transmitted disease (STD). Any sexually active person who has never had any kind of STD is just lucky. He isn't cleaner, smarter, or of higher moral character. Just lucky. But if he remains sexually active, he's greatly increasing his chance of contracting some type of STD at some point in his life. That's because one doesn't choose to get an STD; usually it's your sexual partner who makes the decision for you. Nobody goes out on a date Saturday night saying, "I hope I get herpes tonight." STDs are generally contracted from people who aren't honest about their health or don't have any regard for yours. When you find out, it's too late. This is the very real and sinister underside to our sex-crazed culture.

Actually, herpes is a mild example of what can result from today's sexual encounters. One-sixth of American adults have genital herpes. In addition, there are over 500,000 new cases diagnosed each year. And God knows how many people are never diagnosed or seek treatment. Herpes may hurt like hell, but it isn't fatal. It can be managed with medication and doesn't permanently disrupt a normal life. That's the good news. The bad news is that AIDS is wreaking havoc in our communities, and AIDS kills. It's time to get smart about sex. Our sexually active culture has to face up to the realities of the risks.

Unfortunately this realization came too late for a friend I'll call Mike, who contracted herpes from a woman he met at a party. I'm not happy this happened to him. But I think we can all learn from his example. I still remember Mike's call the morning he had his first outbreak. It was around 3 A.M. when my telephone rang. I buried my ears under my pillow to escape the ringing. But the caller was determined to get my attention. After what seemed like more than a thousand rings, I finally surrendered.

"Hello?" I said, more as a question than a greeting.

"I've got to talk to you, man." Even through my sleep the frantic voice of my friend Mike was recognizable.

Quickly I assessed the situation: 3 A.M. plus Mike on a cellular phone equals a play-by-play description of his booty call. Even half asleep, I knew where this was going. That was the last thing I wanted to hear in the middle of some good sleep. I started thinking of excuses to get off the phone.

"What's up? I have some early appointments tomorrow," I said.

"That chick messed me up, man!" Mike yelled into the phone so hard that his voice turned to static.

"Who did what? I can't keep track of all your women. Which one?"

"The one I met at the party a few weeks ago. The one with the sexy legs."

"Don't tell me she's pregnant," I said, sitting up on the side of the bed.

"No. It's something you wouldn't believe."

"Did she burn you?"

Mike paused and then yelled into the phone again. "Worse! I've got herpes, man. I've got it bad!"

Silence.

"She didn't look like she had herpes," Mike said just above a whisper.

Mike was no different than millions of other men and women; he loved sex. It would be an understatement to say that he was promiscuous. An ideal week for Mike would involve sex with a different woman each night. Some days, he'd lie between the sheets of two or even three different women. Not one of them knowing he'd just rolled out of bed with another woman less than an hour before. His entire emotional well-being depended on the constant consumption of sex. He was an addict. In fact, he probably didn't really know who had given him herpes and couldn't absolutely guarantee that he hadn't already passed it on to someone else.

But don't scream that all men are dogs. It's not only the men. I've heard women brag about such practices as well. They boast about sexing down a man they have on the side and then going home to squeeze in a session from their husband or boyfriend later that same day. They laugh about how they've been able to get away with their schemes for so long. It's not just a male problem. It's a people problem. Promiscuity doesn't have a gender, race, or age.

The Mikes of the world (both male and female) usually know they're skating on thin ice. But they never expect anything to happen to them. It's similar to the attitude we get while watching the evening news. When we see the terrible car crashes, the shootings, and the fires, we keep eating dinner, feeling that those problems are part of the television world and not our own. But just as the world we watch on the news is real, sexually transmitted diseases are real. Did Mike's playing around cost him or was it just a random occurrence? Don't be too quick to nod your head and say God punished him and he deserved it. It could happen to you too. The sexually transmitted diseases of today aren't confined to promiscuous people.

They don't consider your sexual history, lifestyle, public standing, or good deeds. They just strike.

As for his remark about Ms. Sexy Legs not looking like she had herpes, what does an STD look like? There's no certain smile, handshake, or wave to identify someone with an STD. Perhaps there was a day long ago when there were sexually transmitted diseases that only promiscuous people, drug addicts, and unsanitary people carried. But today's diseases are equal opportunity infections. They see no age, race, or economic distinction. They can affect newborn babies and seventy-year-old men just the same. They can strike a sixteen-year-old virgin on her first time or a Beverly Hills gigolo on his thousandth. They can come from a casual lover or a lifelong spouse. You can't tell anything by how a person looks.

Certainly, the probability of contracting such diseases can be reduced by wise sexual practices. But condoms and safe sex don't absolutely eliminate the chance of contracting a sexually transmitted disease. Being highly selective is wise. But the problem remains that every sexual partner you have will not be honest about their sexual or drug use history. And even if they were honest about themselves, they can't verify the sexual and drug use history of all their past partners. Taking it a step further, the partners of that partner can't verify the sexual history of their partners and so on and so on. There's just no guarantee in it anywhere. Condoms are said to be effective. But only if used properly and even they can't be considered totally safe for everything. In short, there's really no way to avoid these diseases other than monogamy or celibacy.

We hear lots of discussion on AIDS and HIV and we should. The number of AIDS cases continues to explode and there's still no cure. Even greater numbers of people continue to be-

come infected with HIV, the virus that causes AIDS, but we
still don't have a vaccine to prevent it.

However, the spectrum of sexually transmitted diseases includes much more than AIDS/HIV. There are other sexually
transmitted diseases to be wary of as well. And they're not as
hard to get as one might imagine. Some of them don't even
require intercourse to be spread. If you're sexually active and
haven't ever encountered any of these diseases, count yourself
as lucky. But remember, it could still happen to you. Don't
develop a false sense of security about STDs. Protect your life
and health by being sexually smart.

AIDS/HIV

What is it?: HIV is the virus that causes AIDS. AIDS is a
group of diseases and symptoms that attack people who are
infected with the HIV virus.

How could I catch it?: Through vaginal, oral, or anal sex
with infected people; or open sores and by transmission of
body fluids. It is believed that AIDS is not spread through sa-
liva.

Where does it affect the body?: The entire body can be
affected by the attack of AIDS on the body's immune system.

What are the symptoms?: People with AIDS/HIV may not
know it for years; they may have no visible symptoms. However, common symptoms of AIDS are fevers, weight loss, fa-
tigue, diarrhea, swollen glands, difficulty maintaining balance,
and difficulty thinking clearly.

What problems does it cause?: After HIV renders the
body's immune system too weak to fight off diseases, AIDS
attacks the body. AIDS is actually a variety of diseases and
symptoms present in the body at once. When these diseases

overwhelm the body's natural defenses, AIDS can be fatal. AIDS can also be passed to babies.

What is the treatment?: Examination and testing by a physician. Though there is promising research being conducted, there is currently no vaccine to prevent HIV; nor is there a cure for AIDS. However, there are some drugs that have helped the body fight AIDS. People living with AIDS wage a daily battle to survive. Some live for years, experiencing up and down cycles in their health, whereas others may suffer slow and painful deaths in relatively short periods of time.

For more discussion on AIDS/HIV, see the chapter "Being Straight About Being Straight."

Gonorrhea

What is it?: A disease caused by a type of bacteria.

How could I catch it?: Through vaginal, oral, or anal sex with infected people.

Where does it affect the body?: The vagina, penis, anus, throat, or eyes, depending on where the infected parts of your partner's body touch yours.

What are the symptoms?: Within a month (usually within five days), painful urination, a puslike discharge, or blood in the urine. **NOTE: Women can carry gonorrhea in the upper part of their vagina without knowing it!**

What problems does it cause?: Without treatment it may cause sterility, pelvic inflammatory disease, or arthritic-type pain in the joints. It can also be passed to babies.

What is the treatment?: Examination and testing by a physician and prescription of antibiotics.

Syphilis
What is it? A disease caused by a type of bacteria.
How can I catch it?: Through vaginal, oral, or anal sex; or intimate skin contact with infected people. Anytime an infected person has open sores, there is a chance of contracting syphilis. **NOTE: Sexual intercourse is not required to catch syphilis!**
Where does it affect the body?: The vagina, penis, anus, mouth, lips, tongue, fingers, chest, eyelids.
What are the symptoms?: Up to a month after infection (typically three to five days), symptoms begin. There are three stages to syphilis: Stage 1. A firm and painless open sore (chancre) forms at the point the infection entered the body.
Stage 2. Approximately six months after the disappearance of the initial sore, more sores occur all over the body along with a skin rash, swollen glands, and bumps on the genitals. There may also be spots on the tongue. Stage 3. This stage can cause serious complications, such as the deformity of skin and bones. It can also cause blindness, heart problems, and brain damage.
What problems does it cause?: Without treatment syphilis may cause skin and bone deformities, blindness, heart problems, and brain damage. It can also infect babies during birth. The open sores associated with syphilis also make it easier to get AIDS.
What is the treatment?: Examination and testing by a physician and prescription of antibiotics.

Genital Herpes
What is it?: Herpes type II is caused by a virus and is generally found on the genitalia. Herpes type I is mainly found on the lips.

How can I catch it?: Through vaginal, oral, or anal sex, kissing, or intimate skin contact. Anytime an infected person has open sores, there is a chance of contracting genital herpes. **NOTE: Sexual intercourse is not required to catch genital herpes!**

Where does it affect the body?: The vagina, penis, anus, lips (cold sores), eyes, almost anywhere on the body.

What are the symptoms?: Within ten days there is an itching, burning sensation on the genitalia followed by painful blisters that eventually disappear. Some people don't have a herpes outbreak for a long period of time (possibly years) after infection. Many people have recurring outbreaks. Some people have only one outbreak of herpes. However, they still carry the virus.

What problems does it cause?: Intense itching and burning, extreme pain, swollen glands, fever, headaches. If located on the cervix, herpes can increase a woman's chance of cancer. Herpes can also be fatal to unborn children. **Women with herpes should seek proper prenatal treatment from a doctor.** The open sores associated with herpes also make it easier to get AIDS.

What is the treatment?: Examination and testing by a physician and management of the blister outbreaks and pain with medications. Currently there is no cure for herpes.

Viral Hepatitis

What is it?: A disease caused by a virus. There are two kinds of viral hepatitis: hepatitis A and hepatitis B. Hepatitis A is usually found in feces. But hepatitis B is found in body fluids, such as those exchanged during sexual intercourse.

How can I catch it?: Vaginal, oral, or anal sex can put you at high risk of contracting hepatitis.

Where does it affect the body?: The liver.

What are the symptoms?: Symptoms of hepatitis B may not start for a few weeks or possibly several months. Symptoms include stomach cramps, nausea, headaches, and vomiting. In the next stage symptoms are swollen glands, liver pain, and yellowish skin and eyes.

What problems does it cause?: Hepatitis B attacks the liver and can be fatal if left untreated. If treated, a person can recover. But there may be some permanent damage to the liver. Some people have recurrences of hepatitis and are never completely cured.

What is the treatment?: Examination and testing by a physician and proper medication. Ask your physician about hepatitis vaccination.

Pubic Lice

What is it?: An infestation by a tiny insect, a condition often referred to as "crabs."

How can I catch it?: Easily through contact with a person who has these insects on their body or from unclean towels or bed linen. **REMINDER: Catching pubic lice doesn't require sexual contact or even skin-to-skin contact!**

Where does it affect the body?: The pubic hair around the genitals.

What are the symptoms?: Usually within a week a person will experience intense itching and skin irritation. One may actually see the tiny insects and their eggs on one's pubic hair.

What problems does it cause?: Possibility of an infection. Mild fever in some cases.

What is the treatment?: See your physician for testing and diagnosis. Treatment for pubic lice is available without a prescription at pharmacies. Usually the treatment involves the application of a shampoo, lotion, or spray. If you follow the directions of the manufacturer, the lice should be killed. It is also important to clean and treat all your clothing, bed, and living areas to kill any lice that may be hiding in those places.

Chancroids

What is it?: A disease caused by a bacterium.

How can I catch it?: Through vaginal, oral, or anal sex, kissing, or skin-to-skin contact with an open sore. **NOTE: Sexual intercourse is not required to get chancroids!**

Where does it affect the body?: The vagina, penis, anus, mouth. Rarely, chancroids occur on other parts of the body.

What are the symptoms?: Within a day or up to a week after infection, a painful open sore forms. **Note: Sometimes women can carry the bacterium that causes chancroids without showing symptoms. However, they can spread the disease to other people.**

What problems does it cause?: Chancroids can spread to other parts of the body. Since chancroids are open sores, they increase the chance of contracting AIDS.

What is the treatment?: Examination and testing by a physician and treatment with antibiotics.

Human Papilloma Virus (Genital Warts)

What is it?: A wart-causing virus.

How can I catch it?: Through vaginal, oral, or anal sex. Also through kissing or intimate skin contact. **NOTE: Sexual intercourse is not required to get the human papilloma virus (HPV).**

Where does it affect the body?: The vagina, penis, anus, or mouth.

What are the symptoms?: The incubation period for vene-

real warts can be a month or perhaps a year. The warts are bumpy and fleshy. They can be small or large and are painless.
What problems does it cause?: The human papilloma virus has been linked to cervical cancer in women. It may also cause cancer of the penis or anus. HPV can also be spread to babies at birth.
What is the treatment?: Examination and testing by a physician. The warts can be removed by your physician.

Chlamydia
What is it?: A disease caused by a bacterium.
How can I catch it?: Through vaginal, anal, or oral sex. Also through intimate skin contact.
Where does it affect the body?: Inside the urethra, in the eyes.
What are the symptoms?: Approximately one to two weeks after infection, there is painful urination, a discharge, and inflammation in the affected genitalia. **NOTE: Chlamydia can be a stealth infection. A person with chlamydia may have no symptoms at all.**
What problems does it cause?: Chlamydia can cause sterility in women. When in the eyes, chlamydia can cause extreme irritation.
What is the treatment?: Examination and testing by a physician and a prescription of antibiotics.

Trichomoniasis
What is it?: Infection with a tiny protozoan.
How can I catch it?: Through vaginal intercourse (including vagina to vagina).
Where does it affect the body?: The vagina, penis.
What are the symptoms?: It is usually women who are in-

fected with trichomonads. Their symptoms typically begin within a month or as little as four days and include an odorous discharge from the vagina, vaginal itching, and inflammation. When men show symptoms of trichomoniasis, there is a discharge from the urethra. **NOTE: Men can carry trichomonads without symptoms.**

What problems does it cause?: Besides being irritating, trichomoniasis has been linked to cervical cancer.

What is the treatment?: Examination and testing by a physician and proper medication.

Source: Centers for Disease Control and Prevention.

POINTS TO REMEMBER

- Every sexually active person is susceptible to getting a sexually transmitted disease, regardless of ethnicity, sex, age, financial status, or sexual preference.
- One can't look at a person and determine if they are infected by an STD.
- Several sexually transmitted diseases can have very serious, even fatal consequences if left untreated.
- You can contract some sexually transmitted diseases from kissing or skin contact. Not all STDs require sexual intercourse for infection.
- Condoms don't provide 100 percent protection against infection by an STD.
- Don't be overcome by the "heat of the moment" and forget about safe, smart sexual practices.
- Don't skip safe, smart sexual practices just because you've been with someone several times.
- Practice safe, smart sex. Get to know people well before becoming intimate with them. You have the right to ask them about their sexual history. Always use condoms and maintain good personal hygiene habits.

A FINAL NOTE: If you even think you may have an STD, see your physician immediately. Most of the STDs discussed above can be cured with early detection. Others must be carefully managed by a physician. Neglecting or postponing treatment of an STD can leave the door open for a serious health problem, infection by other diseases, or HIV.

For more information on sexually transmitted diseases, contact the Centers for Disease Control and Prevention:

The National STD Hotline 1-800-227-8922

How to Have Great Sex

I remember being tired, extremely tired. I thought I could gain some energy by closing my eyes for a moment. But when I closed them, time stopped. I wasn't resting my eyes, I was asleep. It was good sleep too. Then I heard a sigh and felt her body stirring under me. My eyes popped open. I remembered where I was and what I was doing. I was having sex. How could I fall asleep while having sex? Was there something wrong with me?

Actually, there was nothing wrong with me. I just needed some sleep, not sex. But instead of going to sleep when I came home from work that night, I felt compelled to have sex. This was for no other reason than the fact that it had been over a week since my last erotic encounter. When I was in my late twenties I thought I would quickly go insane if I didn't have a steady diet of female bodies. I don't like the term "dog." It dehumanizes men. But I have to admit there was a time I felt like a dog. Not in the sense that I didn't have feelings for women. But more in the sense that I was serving my sex drive the way a dog serves its master.

Back then, checking my answering machine was always a thrill, because I was willing to play the role of boy toy for women who were interested. When women called, their messages were coded in casual innuendos, "I'm off tomorrow . . . ," "I'll be in Houston through Friday . . . ," "I'm bored . . ." To which I always responded faithfully. My body was ready to play with women as long as they didn't want anything more than a hot quickie. I was happy bouncing from bed to bed as a terminally uncommitted bachelor. I thought I was living the good life.

In reality, I was a man out of control. I could be reading a book in the solitude of my living room. I could be in the middle of a movie. I could be nodding off to sleep. But if the phone would ring with an offer, I was up and out the door. But I wasn't satisfied. I felt that I never had enough new prospects. I was always hunting for more women everywhere I went. For example, when I went grocery shopping, I'd look for women up and down each aisle, flirt with the cashier, and hunt in the parking lot too. It got so bad that I started keeping prewritten love notes in my back pocket. These generic, no-name notes consisted of a few blank compliments that could be made to any woman in any situation. I was obsessed. I lived with the fear that if I didn't hunt, I was going to miss something. And I believed that whatever that something was, it was better than anything I'd had before.

The question is, what was I afraid I was going to miss? Slowly the answer was coming to me, because I was growing tired of the hunt. I wanted to be able to actually walk out my door and not be a slave to my libido. I wanted to get calls but not feel compelled to respond. The seeds for my healing were already within. I began to dislike what I was doing. I just did it because I hadn't ever given myself the courage and permission to let go and live my life according to the voice I heard inside. The voice that constantly told me I would be happier if I could harness my lusts and connect with love. Like so many people, I was blindly following a role. The part I played was that of the young swinging bachelor. I was doing what I thought I was supposed to do. But not thinking about what I wanted to do. My mind was on remote control.

It all came together in the moment I fell asleep during sex.

When I woke up, I knew that I was going to have to change my sexual habits. I was finally tired of disrespecting my body. It was time to unplug from the stereotypes about bachelorhood that made me think I was just a toy to be used for physical pleasure. The body is sacred. It is a temple for the spirit. But I had been desecrating my own sacred temple through my actions. I doubt if my sexual partner that night knew what she was doing to herself either. It was spiritual blindness on both our parts.

That night set me on a new course in life. I was ready for spiritual advancement. But I needed some way to have closure with where I'd come from, or I wouldn't evolve any further. That meant I had to gain power over my passions. To do that, I took what was an extremely drastic move for me at that time. With the hope that I would gain spiritual vision, I decided to go on a sexual fast. I told only a couple of my friends what I was planning to do. One friend thought it was a well-intended but unworkable idea. The other one thought I'd lost my mind. I wasn't sure about my sanity at that point either. I knew I was right in what I was doing. But spending days and nights of bachelorhood on a sexual fast felt like a type of social sacrilege.

Adjustment to this drastic change of lifestyle came with difficulty. Going cold turkey made me feel as though I was holding my breath. I thought I could only abstain for a short time. It even seemed to me that what I was doing was violating a basic law of nature. But it didn't take long for me to see that I wasn't violating any biological laws by avoiding sexual encounters. My body wasn't suffering withdrawal. Nothing had changed. After I made it through the first few weeks, I realized that I didn't actually need sex to survive. That was my turning point. Closing that door allowed another to open. With my nights free, I discovered a treasure of time that could be spent on me. I had time to do more things I enjoyed. This included writing more.

All this happened in the early and middle part of 1996, when I completed and self-published the best-selling original version of this book. I would never have had time to put that project together if I hadn't found some closure with my over-sexed past. That lifestyle had been draining my time and energy. It was only through my new outlook that I was free to invest my time in things that would benefit me. I remember how creating *Brothers, Lust, and Love* became my passion. I worked on it late at night, early in the morning, and any other time I could steal from my day job.

But still the old habits proved to be a strong test of my willpower. To be perfectly honest, I faltered a few times during my sexual fast. But I can also honestly say it was more mental than physical. The most difficult obstacle to overcome was my mental weakness. In fact, during the hardest part of my cold-turkey shock, I compromised and told myself that I would keep myself on hold just long enough to write the book and then dive back into action. But, thank God, things worked out differently. As I wrote the book and delved deeper and deeper into the mysteries of myself, my words became a self-discovery, an extended self-therapy.

My life was changing as it unfolded on the pages in front of me. But no transformation is complete without tests. The phone continued to ring, and I continued to get seductive messages. But I had grown much stronger. Before I knew it, three months had passed. After that period of time, I felt liberated from my libido. It was as if I went through a tunnel and came out into the light on the other side. Then the three months turned to six. No sex and I hadn't lost my mind as a result. In fact it wasn't as hard as I'd thought it would be. I was enjoying my new freedom, found in sexless living. With control over my sex drive, I had given myself a power that I previously thought to be unattainable.

I had closed my eyes, fallen backward, and expected faith to save me. It did, and I gained power from it. That power led to a new focus in my life. My new focus was on my overall wellness: mental, physical, and spiritual. Everything I did now was in a new light. Since my body was a sacred temple, I had to act as though it was. That meant I had to be much more careful of where I put my body. Whom I made love to was no longer a sporting event. I resolved that the next time my temple was joined with another, it would be in love, not lust. I was chilled by the thought of all the times I risked sexually transmitted disease. I was chilled by the thought of how much of my sacred seed I had put into women with whom I had shared nothing sacred. But I was finally free, no longer thinking from below the belt. All this new thinking didn't mean I wasn't looking at women. I just had it in perspective. I no longer felt compelled to make a move on anyone who looked good. At last, I didn't feel as though I was missing out.

After putting sex in perspective, I was able to meet a woman and clearly see her spirit first. By creating a spiritual bond we were then able to create the right kind of love. From there, all other things came naturally, in their proper space and time, including great sex. I finally realized that spiritually based relationships didn't have to be boring. On the contrary, I learned that centering a relationship in God's realities, instead of physical illusions, made things all the better. But getting to that place was a long and twisted road. It's amazing to look back at the chain of seemingly ironic events and how they all connected to make something good happen. For it was not by hunting women that I kept myself from missing what I thought I was searching for. It was the *hunt* itself that was the culprit. While I was on the hunt I couldn't discern the truth from the blur my own life had become. What I needed was clear vision through my spiritual eye, which came only after I made the sacrifice to attain it. It turned out that my joke about lack of sex causing insanity was another example of my ironic odyssey. The real insanity was the spiritual blindness that resulted from too much sex. It turns out that my greatest sexual experience was to not have sex at all. Not having sex liberated my mind. I realized once and for all that sex was a gift meant to be shared in love.

THINGS TO THINK ABOUT

1. Do you have a healthy control of your sex drive or does sex drive you?

2. Have you ever grown tired of sex? Were you OK with that feeling?

3. Have you ever been celibate for a short period of time? A long period of time? If yes, how did you feel and what were the benefits?

4. Is there too much emphasis on sex in relationships? Or, is the role of sex in a relationship misunderstood?

LOVE

I Want Your Soul

The most skillful lover is one who would never have to touch a woman's body. The man who could excite and satisfy her senses on a higher level. This seems to be a contradiction. But if making love is ultimately a bonding, a fusing of energies, why are bodies necessary? The time outside the bedroom leads to the passion within. Touching, crazy fun times, and the quiet evenings of doing nothing at all create the intimacy found in lovemaking. Discovering and loving a woman's soul is the first step on the journey to true passion.

As a boy, I didn't know what making love was. It was a foreign concept. I supposed it was some aberration of the four-letter word we etched on bathroom walls. I was the typical example of a boy with exploding hormones. All of us were hunting the girls at school as if we were wolves. We had no understanding of the explosive physiology taking hold of our young bodies. We didn't know the first thing about linking those physical changes to the abstract thoughts of love, romance, and passion.

What we learned about love and sex came from other guys. We didn't ask the girls what they liked. We asked each other. My mentor was an eighth-grade boy. He was cool, a starter on the varsity football squad, and older than I was. As far as I was concerned, all those things made him an expert on sex too. He told me what women liked and didn't like. He'd even had sex already. That alone made me revere his words. In turn, I passed those myths to the boys in my circle of friends, and they passed them on as well. But not one of us knew what we were talking about. Not even the mentor.

In reality, the most I'd seen of a woman's body was an accidental glimpse of my mother getting dressed for work. My only other images came when my buddy would steal a *Playboy* magazine from his dad's collection. We'd huddle in his garage and gawk at the naked women on the pages. Occasionally we'd get an additional treat. Someone's older brother would give us a real account from his sex life. He'd call it like a basketball game. We'd get so excited that we would barely hear the entire story. But amid all the whooping, hollering, and hand-slapping, we never learned about the feelings involved. As a result, our minds were being shaped to define sex in terms of games and competitive conquests.

Though misinformed, all of us eventually found our way into the lives of girls who, like us, were experiencing the hormone explosions of adolescence. Our first sexual experiences were clandestine. There was the fake Monday-morning killer stomachache. It was the big one that had you buckled over and rolling on the floor. When our parents left, we walked around the corner to the house of a girl who had also happened to stay home that day due to "illness." Some guys tried to date. But when their skinnin' and grinnin' "Yes sir"'s and "no sir"'s fell on the distrustful ears of suspicious fathers, other means had to be employed. We became skilled at scrambling in and out of windows by cover of night. We knew that it was risky business. But it was all worth it to boys seeking to satisfy an urge. With these girls, we tested our misinformed theories and followed the advice of our mentors. No doubt they were following the poor advice of older girls who had misinformed them too.

In the ninth grade, I fell in love. For the first time, I'd felt a lump in my throat instead of my pants. It was something new and exciting. When I looked at her, I didn't glue my eyes to her body. Instead I was filled with emotion. It was a strange sensation, both glorious and frightening. The friend with whom I gawked over stolen copies of *Playboy* was experiencing the same feeling with another girl. We talked about it and couldn't believe it. When we were with these girls, we didn't think about sex first. We had another feeling, and it felt good. Although my puppy love affair didn't last, I had been bitten by the love bug. Once bitten, one never recovers. I wanted more of that feeling. But it was elusive because I didn't really understand what it was and where it came from.

"Tell me you love me." Words escaping on a whisper from a woman beneath my body. I didn't love her. For me there was nothing there more than the connection of our bodies. Lacking love, I had turned to fulfillment through lust. I had developed a sophisticated philosophy of separating sex from love. I couldn't understand why the women I was dating couldn't see that as clearly as I did. My thinking on that subject led to some painful misunderstandings. I was deaf to the requests of women for more than sex. When it was time to do things out of bed, I was nowhere to be found or always busy. It has always been hard for me to accept that there was a time when I played games with the love of others by being selfish and callous. But I did.

Eventually I had enough of the sour endings to leave me pondering my ways. A mature man doesn't take sex and leave a hollow and hurt woman behind. Making love is special to him because he is giving himself in the process. I didn't learn that as a boy sneaking in and out of bedroom windows.

Sex isn't a toy. You can do it in the car, on the kitchen counter, in the park, at the beach, standing, sitting, kneeling, with honey, body oil, whipped cream, strawberries, peaches, etc. But one day the thrill will be gone. I was left with a feeling that I wanted more than what a body could offer. But I couldn't identify that need without some real soul-searching. I finally realized that making love wasn't a physical act, but one of spiritual bonding.

I've used and hurt some women out there, and I've been used and hurt as well. Those experiences helped me see that love and sex, though separated in the harsh realities of our society, are inseparable in concept. I realized that to make love to a woman I needed to love her. Gone forever was the horny kid who sought the adventure of a quick thrill. Born was a man seeking a soulful connection.

Now I try to avoid the pure lust of bodies; instead I seek to match spirits. I can't spiritually connect with every woman I meet. Therefore, I don't sleep with every woman I meet. Now I want to find my soul mate and make love to her. I don't know what she looks like. I can't describe a face, skin, hair, height, or build. But that isn't necessary for me to have a fantasy about this woman. Closing my eyes, I can imagine touching her slowly in a room with the smell of incense filling the darkness. I feel myself licking red wine from her body as the taste mixes with her juices on my tongue. We join into a secret sensual rhythm. Our dance takes us into a world of tingling sensations, bodies sensitive to the slightest touch, sound, and taste. We move slowly, feeling the rhythms of our spirits. My brow is wet with the sweet sweat of our passions. I become intoxicated with her. Our senses explode. She gasps and wraps tightly around me, sinking her fingers into my shoulders. I fill the hunger in her body with my soul.

I whisper to my lover in the heat of the darkness, "I don't want your body. I want your soul."

THINGS TO THINK ABOUT

1. As a teenager, what were your ideas about sex?
2. As an adult, how have your views on sex changed?
3. Do you view sex as only a physical activity, like a sport? Or do you view sex as a spiritual connection?
4. Does every love affair have to culminate in a sexual experience?

Nothing to Fear

Sprawled across the couch, I gazed up at the ceiling. My body was limp and torqued, a reflection of my twisted state of mind. Six months after I pushed her away and time *hadn't* healed my wounds, I realized what I had done.

I don't have a problem with communicating. I can say "I'm sorry" one hundred times. I can say, "I love you" one hundred times. I can surprise a woman with roses, chocolates, and love notes. External expressions through words, sounds, and actions have never been a problem for me. Instead, my problem is a fear of being hurt in love. A fear that is not always evident to others, but battles inside me.

Both men and women have to face the fact that intimacy doesn't come easily. But with men, it is more difficult. Quite frankly, intimacy scares the hell out of me and lots of other men. If intimacy were just wine, candlelight, and making love all night, it wouldn't be frightening. But it's so much more than that. Intimacy is a state achieved when lovers come together and create an energy greater than themselves. To attain intimacy, we have to follow the lead of our emotions into a world of the unknown. For most men, the act of handling these uncharted emotions is intimidating.

Little boys are made of snails, frogs, and puppy-dog tails. Little girls are made of sugar, spice, and everything nice. Boys wear blue. Girls wear pink. Girls cry. Boys don't. As children, we grew up with a strict social protocol. A protocol we often learned from the games we played. Unfortunately for boys, the games we played didn't teach us how to handle the emotions we'd need to be men in love. It was different for the girls. They didn't spend all of their time playing with dolls, learning to bake cookies, and screaming about the Jackson 5. They also spent lots of time talking. Through that talking they learned to open up and experience their feelings and emotions, and to share them with others. Meanwhile, we boys were outside playing basketball, wrestling in the grass, and running footraces across the vacant lot next door.

As boys, the relationship we had with our emotions was totally different. Early on, we learned that there was a limited range of appropriate emotions for boys to express. Joy and happiness were expressed through yelling or victory chants after winning a game. Anger and frustration were vented through a hard tackle on the football field or clenched fists; feelings of warmth and closeness were communicated through hand slaps and pats on the back for the guy who scored the winning basket. Unlike the girls, boys didn't hug. It wasn't appropriate to touch another boy in a display of emotion. Unlike the girls, our conversations were usually shallow. Being too eager to have deep conversations about anything other than sports, cars, or girls was frowned upon. Boys usually stayed on the surface of issues, in the comfort zone.

For example, when I played Little League football, it was extremely important not to show any pain, fear, or cowardice. I was brawny for my age and accustomed to facing-off on the grass against boys who were older, bigger, faster, and stronger than I was. But I was still expected to do my job on the line. I was expected to take my opponent's ground, or at the very least hold mine. One afternoon, I and a much older boy who was as strong as a bull battled on the line. Finally, toward the end of the game, I grew weary and he got the best of me.

When the quarterback called the audible, the other kid exploded into motion, knocking me off-balance. Then he stepped on my hand with his cleats.

Although the pain was terrible, I held it in. My family was there. My neighbors were there. My friends were along the sidelines. The girls from school were there. I couldn't show pain. This was an important lesson as part of my induction into the male fraternity. Men never show pain. Pain is an emotion. To show emotion is to exhibit weakness. From boyhood, we have learned to hide our emotions.

How, then, can we men achieve intimacy when we don't feel comfortable with our feelings? All of us deal with it in different ways. Some men just never admit their feeling-phobia. Instead, they deny having feelings. They claim they just can't settle down with one woman. But this very mentality of "getting around" actually requires a man to realize that he *does* have feelings. Realizing his vulnerability to those feelings, he runs from them. As a general rule, the more a man gets around sexually, the lonelier that man really is on the inside. This man fears the mirror. He doesn't want to see himself because he won't like the image staring back at him. Looking into the mirror is a playboy. Reflecting back at him is the face of that scared little boy facing the giant on the football field. This time the giant is an albatross of emotions that he can't get a handle on. It's easier to hit and run. To stay in the streets and never have feelings.

Another popular excuse is the career. Some of us dodge intimacy by claiming we don't have the time for a wife or steady girlfriend. We say we're on the fast track and a woman just wouldn't understand the hectic schedule, the business trips, female associates, etc. It's a great excuse to hide behind. There's nothing wrong with a man's building a career. But behind the facade of business, he's still a human being. He still knows the hollow cold of loneliness and the desire to feel the warmth of a woman in his life. He just finds a means to cope with it—his work. The overdriven career man successfully hides himself behind his work, his demanding schedule. No time to talk. No time to listen. No time to feel. He's safe.

"I don't want to be hurt again." Other men have made the mistake of holding the current woman in their life hostage for the actions of another. This is one more great excuse to use when the subject of commitment arises. We just say, "I don't want to be hurt again," and run behind a rock to hide. I was guilty of that one. In a relationship, I dragged in the emotional baggage from a previous relationship that had gone sour, and used it as an excuse to keep my distance. But using that excuse destroyed the current relationship.

I remember it clearly. I left her after an argument. But something was missing inside me. Something I had to go back for. That longing to go and get what was missing woke me early one morning in a state of emotional vertigo. I knew I couldn't go on running from my own shadow. I faced myself and admitted that I was insecure. The torturous demon in my life was not a femme fatale; it was the insecurity dwelling inside me. At some time during my attempts to remain emotionally distant, I had crossed the line from lover to being in love with this woman. That situation involving feelings I hadn't planned for.

I analyzed why I had driven her out of my life. Why had I met her every effort at intimacy with venom? It seemed that the closer we'd become, the more distant I'd wanted to be. I hadn't trusted the feelings I had. Because my own insecurities had begun to overtake me, I'd begun to take it out on her. I'd thrown everything at her that I could: accusations of cheating, instant arguments, cross-examinations of her every action. All because I hadn't been able to handle what I felt.

All those things came back and rushed through my mind as I lay in bed analyzing why I'd driven my girlfriend away after a year of being with her. I wanted to call her, but it was 4 A.M. I closed my eyes and tried to sleep. But she haunted me. I could feel her breasts against my bare chest. I tasted her tongue. I could imagine my hand tracing the curves of her body. I still wanted her. But I snapped to reality. I knew that before I could make love to her again, I had to become secure in my own ability to love. I had to learn that making love was not a physical act, but a climax of the very emotions of which I was afraid.

To this woman, I could have bared my soul. A woman who made me laugh and held my head to her bosom when I cried. That's why I'd found fault with her. She could touch the inside of me. She moved my spirit and that terrified me. That's why I'd pushed her away. I realized that to gain in love, I had to feel. I had to expose myself and be vulnerable. That was something I couldn't accept. I feared the vulnerability created by my emotions. Yet I yearned for the intimacy that could only be gained through those emotions.

Admitting my problem was just the first step. I faced myself and confessed that I was afraid of intimacy—a revelation that came quickly after accepting the fact that I had been mindlessly jumping from woman to woman after the relationship had ended. I was searching for someone with whom I'd feel comfortably neutral. Someone with whom I wouldn't feel vulnerable. In essence, I wanted to have love without the vulnerability of experiencing any feelings. I tried to cheat love at its own game. I found myself falling into a destructive and hollow pattern. I would meet a woman, fall deeply in *like* with her, search for happiness between her sheets, and bail out of the back door before daylight. For some, that sounds like a good night, a good score. But it's not safe physically or emotionally. For the emotionally mature—or those who, like me, *want* to be mature— there's a lonely-hearted conclusion to that story. One gains a numb satisfied body that diminishes into a lonely spirit.

After accepting my problem, I felt I owed my estranged girlfriend an explanation. The next night I drove to her house to explain it all to her. I was taking a risk because I was uninvited, but I figured if she were with someone else, it would be poetic justice. I would just have to live with the consequences. Luckily, she was alone. She cracked the door open and peered out at me in curious confusion. I was pathetic. I was just another apologizing man. It was the same old story line—a man screws up and comes back to the scene of his love crime expecting to be forgiven.

I popped the roses in front of me, making my intentions clear. After all I'd done, she still loved me. It was in her eyes. The emotions were swelling inside me and I felt intimidated again. Her ability to love was larger than my entire presence at her doorstep. The warmth in her eyes made me want to cry. But instead, I was macho man. I cried *inside*. For a change, I didn't know what to say. Words didn't come easily. They didn't come at all. How could I tell her I was afraid of intimacy?

Our encounter ended as awkwardly as it started. No kisses or hugs were exchanged. No promises were made. We simply embraced with our glances and restrained our emotions. As I stood there, I hoped my eyes were saying what my mouth couldn't, because I was unable to find the right words to express my fear of intimacy to her. But I left as a more mature man. I hoped it wasn't too late for us. But more importantly, I had grown. And that's what life is about: growth and spiritually perfecting ourselves.

Though I never found the right words, I did find something else in myself that night. I confronted a problem that had imprisoned my emotions and threatened to sabotage every relationship in my future, including the relationship I have with myself. But after that moment of awkward silence with her, I was on my way to discovering the intimacy that brings about male-female friendship, a wholesome exchange of feelings, and a sincere desire for monogamous love. That night didn't cure my intimacy phobia. But I had found the way to begin to recover from my fear of intimacy. I had found and embraced the feelings inside me. That was the beginning. I know I have many more steps to go, but I'll get there.

I want to love. I will love.

THINGS TO REMEMBER

1. Why do you think men have difficulty accepting their emotions?
2. Does our society encourage men to resist their feelings?
3. Why shouldn't we tell boys they can cry?
4. Can women do anything to help men overcome fears of their feelings?

Making Love from the Inside Out

"You stick it in her real hard and go uh, uh, uh, as fast as you can." As little boys, that's what we imagined making love was all about. But many grown men have been accused of not having a clue as to what should be going on in the bedroom.

Some men aren't comfortable with themselves sexually. Some have problems showing sensitivity. Others take their egos into the bedroom. Then there are those who see sex as a power struggle. I remember seeing a clean-cut young professional-looking brother at the bookstore one Saturday evening. I was behind him in line. As we both looked around, our eyes met and I tried to kick him a "what's up?" head nod, but he quickly turned away. *What's wrong with this brother?* I thought. Being nosy, I glanced over his shoulder at the book he slid across the counter to the girl at the register. It was *The New Joys of Sex*.

Then I realized he probably felt a little ashamed being caught buying such a book. His body language said it all. Maybe he was afraid I thought he was a weak man because he was reading a book on how to make love. Shouldn't a real man just naturally have lovemaking talent? No is the answer and I wish I had a dollar for every man who thought he did. Or I wish I had a nickel for every time a man thought he was ringing the bell and was really just tapping on the door. Based on what the women say, I'd be rich ten times over.

The key to making love lies far beyond the obvious. But to learn exactly what makes sex pleasurable we have to unlearn much of what we have been taught. We must eliminate the idea of sex being just a physical quick thrill. We have to elevate sex to a more sacred experience. Sex expresses bonding and togetherness. That's why the good physical feeling it gives is not enough in itself. That's why we all still yearn for more from each other. The reason for those desires lies in the most basic elements of our existence. Actually, we're more spiritual than physical. It is not really the touch that we long for. Sexual contact in it's purest form is spiritual. It's two spirits reaching forward to join together as one. Some cultures recognize the union of mental, physical, and spiritual bonding that is represented in sex. The ancient Hindu Tantric philosophy recognizes sex as a sacred act. The ancient Chinese Taoist philosophy views sex spiritually. Traditional Judeo-Christian beliefs revere the act of lovemaking as a bond so sacred that it is only to be shared between husband and wife. But the sacred nature of sex is an old belief that we seemed to have cast away in our modern world.

The brother I saw reading the book was undoubtedly on some sort of road to self-discovery. He was probably trying to graduate from simply having sex to learning how to make a higher connection. And that is a learned skill, such as reading and riding a bicycle. He should feel no shame for wanting to know how to touch, caress, and make love to a woman to bring her to the full culmination of her passion. He has probably come full circle and knows that there is more to pleasing a woman than groping, grunting, and pulsating in the dark. Making love to a woman is a mysterious spiritual experience. For that very reason, a man doesn't need to have five or six women. It could take him all of his life to learn to fulfill just one woman.

Sex starts in the head, not in the bed. The most sexually

alluring thing about a woman is her mind. When a woman shares her thoughts, dreams, and fears with a man, she is sharing her whole being, not just her body. It is essential to take time to get to know a woman and learn to appreciate her for who she is. Fellas, go beyond the body and try to understand her soul.

So then, how do you make love to a woman? Since each woman is unique, there's no scientific formula. Each woman must be explored as an individual. But there are some things every man must know. First, to be a good lover, a man must be comfortable with himself and his own body. He must know that a woman has five senses to please and his lovemaking should excite those senses. He must be able to be both dominant and submissive, hard and soft, powerful and vulnerable. Above all, a man should love a woman from the inside out. He must first love her mind and spirit. Only then can he touch her body in the most intimate of ways.

THREE WAYS TO MAKE LOVE FROM THE INSIDE OUT (THE THREE T'S)

When men are discovering ways to love a woman from the inside out, they must remember to keep the focus on the mental and physical aspects of a woman's sexuality. Sexual satisfaction is about more than flavored massage oils, new positions, licking whipped cream or honey from a woman's body, having sex in unusual places, sex toys, etc. No matter how adventurous sex gets, it still leaves a desire for something more. That's because we'll never be completely satisfied with just the physical aspect of sex, because sex that doesn't involve

POINTS TO REMEMBER

- Making love is a spiritual act, not just a physical thrill.
- Men who desire to become better lovers should first learn to love, respect, and appreciate the woman with whom they want to make love.
- Being a good lover isn't a natural skill; lovemaking is something we learn.
- Men should read books on female sexuality and lovemaking to get a better understanding about the sexuality of women. But men should not limit their study of female sexuality to techniques for physical sexual satisfaction. Instead, they should focus on how a woman's sexuality is an extension of her mind and spirit. Men can find many good books available at bookstores and libraries on the subject of female sexuality and lovemaking. Also, good sources of information on what women want from men are women's magazines such as *Essence, Black Elegance,* and *Today's Black Woman.* (See the section of this chapter "Three Ways to Make Love from the Inside Out.")
- Men who want to become better lovers should ask their significant other how they can enhance their lovemaking. But for a man to ask a woman how he can be a better lover, a man must be open-minded and put his ego aside. Likewise, the woman should realize how vulnerable such a question makes a man feel and be careful not to insult him. Her answers should come from a standpoint of love, not criticism or ridicule. She needs to realize that a man has taken a great risk with his feelings by asking a woman how he can become a better lover.
- Women want to be desired for who they are as people, not only for their sex appeal.
- Lovemaking is a three-dimensional experience integrating mind, body, and spirit.

the mind and soul is incomplete. That's the reason some men are never satisfied and always looking for more sex; they're not getting the full experience that comes from making a soul-to-soul connection with their partner. To be completely satisfying, sex has to start on the inside and work its way out to the physical body. Our bodies can only be satisfied when our minds and souls are first satisfied.

But how do we get to that soul-to-soul level? How do we go from just having sex to making love? The answer is: by starting to love a woman's mind and soul. Here are three simple suggestions for men who want to make love from the inside out:

1. TALKING
Conversation is a path that leads into a woman's mind and soul. The best way for a man to make a soul-to-soul connection with a woman is through conversation. I'm not referring to blank flirtations, but meaningful conversations. Meaningful conversations are the ones in which men and women share themselves and explore new areas of each other. In those casual conversations, things flow easily from one subject to another; one moment you could be talking about art, then politics, and then your favorite movie or even the weather. A good conversation is like dancing, it flows and feels good from the inside out. Through talking and relating, men and women can become much closer in mind and spirit than they ever could by sex alone.

2. TOUCHING
Everyone is familiar with touching in a sexual way. But what about nonsexual touching? Caressing, snuggling, hugging, and massaging without a sexual intent is a great way to build a spiritual and mental bond with a woman. Sex is not the only

form through which men and women can feel passion. Try an
evening of nonsexual touching with your significant other. It
could be something simple such as renting movies and snuggling on the couch, or brushing her hair or rubbing her feet.
Or it could be something more sensual, such as giving the
woman you love a full body massage.

3. TANTALIZING

Men who tantalize the minds and souls of women they love
know that small things are important steps to the passion that
culminates in the physical act of making love. There are many
ways men can tantalize women, two of them have already been
discussed: conversation and nonsexual touching. Other subtle
ways a man can tantalize a woman's mind are: his cologne, his
voice, clothing that accentuates his features, a special way in
which he hugs the woman he loves, etc. Some women say they
are tantalized by a man's overall personality; traits such as confidence, intelligence, and sensitivity are sexy to many women.

Love on Condition

The diamonds of her wedding ring didn't shimmer in the darkness. As we sat in the flickering candlelight, the rules of society were slowly and deliberately being blurred to mean nothing. We both knew the dangers of our dinner in the dark corner. It was far too compromising a place for the reunion of a single man and an unhappily married woman who had been lovers before the ring was placed on her finger.

As I helped her into her overcoat, there was a battle going on in my mind. I had loved her. Now I lusted after her. I dreaded the moment she would finish slipping into her coat and turn around. I was afraid of what I might say or do. She turned and looked into my eyes, completing the thought for me. "The traffic is bad. I don't want to go home now. Could I come over for a while?" she asked.

We sat in my living room talking and laughing. But she suspended the fun with a moment of seriousness. Her words were like a disclaimer, an announcement to set boundaries within the land of broken rules into which we had wandered. "I love my husband. He's good to me. I married him because I knew he could take care of me, and he has. Being with another man doesn't mean I don't love him. A person can love different people in different ways." I sensed something profound behind her words, but I pushed them to the back of my mind. I preferred to ignore them in my moment as predator.

As the setting sun left my living room in darkness, she lay her head against my shoulder. I touched her. A forbidden touch. I kissed her with a forbidden kiss. Suddenly the words of love and respect for her husband were pushed into the distance by her hunger to be kissed. She acted as though the heat of another body energized her and made her stronger. She was ravenous and seemed to consume me. *How can she love him and do this?* I thought. I was a willing participant. I had done nothing to prevent this from happening. Any condemning words I might have said would've made me part of the chorus of hypocrites in this world who carry on in the darkness and point fingers of accusation in the light. My question was not one of judgment or condemnation, but naive curiosity. How could a married person do this?

Years later, her ideas continued to resound through my head. She loved her husband but still came to me time after time. Different love for different people? Love for more than one person? Back then, it was hard for me to understand or believe. I thought she was just making excuses. I thought she was trying to convince herself that our affair was justified by some idealistic code of love. But for years after we stopped seeing each other, I heard the echo of her words: *A person can love different people in different ways.* That statement kept coming back, until I understood it.

The love we give and receive is usually a less than perfect, conditional love. People generally love something about you or something you can do for them. I love you because you're beautiful . . . I love your body . . . I love you because you can take care of me . . . I love sex with you . . . I love you because you give me attention . . . I love you because you understand me . . . We give and receive an imperfect form of love based on conditions.

Unfortunately, human beings have great difficulty separating love from conditions. The question of whom we love is often clouded by what use a person has to us. It has more to do with suppressing love for someone who doesn't meet our criteria at the cost of acquiring something we need. Therein lies the problem. When we push love to the bottom for the sake of gaining other things, our need to love and be loved will remain and resurface. When our feelings of love aren't met by the person in our life, we seek it elsewhere. The lines become blurred and we create conditional love based solely upon what someone can do for us, based upon how they can fill a particular need we have.

Ms. Right is raised to marry Mr. Right. Likewise, Mr. Right was groomed to marry a princess. The conditions for their love often include good looks, strong earning potential, imported cars, and pretty friends cloned to be just like them. The erroneous conclusion that follows is that surely two people so similar are right for each other and can live happily ever after in their contrived world.

But what happens when Mr. and Ms. Right don't work out? When fate deals them tough cards at the table? What happens when problems that challenge the conditions of their love start to pop up? Statistics tell us that almost half of all marriages are on their way to divorce as soon as the vows are spoken. So many seemingly perfect couples go astray. So many storybook romances don't have a happy ending.

In fitting our lives together we often forget to factor in the elements of spirit necessary to sustain a long relationship. We calculate combined incomes. We carefully forecast a ten-year plan complete with children, cars, homes, and vacations. The focus becomes what we can do for and with each other, rather than how we feel about each other. The love, feelings, and spiritual connection are at best suppressed and at worst ignored.

So many of us actually don't know any better than to have superficial conditions for love. Too many mothers tell their

daughters to go for the money. Too many fathers tell their sons
to go for the looks. Ms. Right's mother told her to marry a
good man; a doctor, lawyer, executive, or architect. Mr.
Right's parents told him to marry a *good* woman; an attractive
woman from a *good* family. Mr. and Ms. Right are just repeat-
ing the patterns instilled in them. Patterns life will often prove
to be wrong and useless.

Later, when the perfection blows up in their faces, they'll
wonder what happened. We ask why, and nobody has a good
answer, so we blame relationships and marriage. There are
skeptics of marriage and long-term relationships who contend
that such arrangements are antiquated concepts that we
shouldn't carry into the twenty-first century. They contend
that committed relationships are a useless part of a pestering
morality that hinders the free thinking of contemporary men
and women by lading them with guilt for having the natural
biological urge to roam.

But there's nothing wrong with love. It's as strong today as
it's ever been. It hasn't fallen victim to any new philosophies.
We just don't listen to it. The fault lies within us. Love is still
pure. But, of course, even pure love has conditions. However,
they don't include physical, material, or financial things. The
conditions of love are emotional, spiritual, and sensual. We
make ourselves unhappy by complicating the process with our
lesser conditions. We often try to build a bridge between emotional happiness and material comfort—a bridge that can't exist. It's certainly possible to have them both, but they are not
inherently elements of one another. They are as different as
black and white, hot and cold, day and night. Seeking love
based on material conditions will lead to a dead end. But seeking the spiritual conditions of love will continue to open new
doors and take a person to higher heights.

In the case of my former love, she had once been a struggling single mother with a need for security. He was older, established, and stable. She admitted to falling in love with the security he could provide first, and him second. She felt she had to make the choice to marry in order to survive. Before she met her husband she had dropped out of college to work full-time. She was barely able to pay for rent and day care. Every morning she had to pray that her rickety old Volkswagen Rabbit would run. Six months after meeting her husband, she was living in a fine suburban home, back in school full-time, and driving a new Volvo. Her husband even picked up the tab for day care.

But in a short time, both her emotional needs and physical desires were unmet. She and her husband hardly talked. He rarely made time for her. He was physically distant and emotionally aloof. But they had met all of the other conditions for each other. She wanted security. He wanted a young beautiful trophy wife. Soon she found herself feeling neglected, unattractive, and even undesirable. She thought I could make her feel better. She wanted me to restore her self-esteem.

But we tried to fix the problem the wrong way. My lust and her desire to be loved collided. For her, it was time to bravely face the problems in her life, and find the answer within herself. If I were really being a friend, I would've helped her discover that. She needed affirmation, inspiration, and the listening ear of a friend. At the time, I was immature. Now I know mistakes, tragedies, and missed opportunities all have to be recycled into learning experiences. Her words that night in my living room slammed my naiveté about love into the brick wall of reality. I did learn.

I learned that in this world, love grows only after our conditions are met. The conditions of some are often lofty and noble while others are predatory and selfish. It's a less than perfect love designed for a less than perfect world. Our conditions for love are created to satisfy our minds, to rationalize the lusts in our hearts, and to explain the forces acting upon us that we can't see or understand. It's not pure love. It's not perfect. It's not right. But it's the way things are in this world.

THINGS TO THINK ABOUT

1. What are your conditions for love? Are they physical characteristics, material items, or are they spiritually based?

2. Have you ever been in a relationship in which someone loved something about you more than he/she loved you? What was it (sex, money, a place to stay, etc.)?

3. Looking back on your past, have you ever been involved with someone because you loved what he/she could do for you?

4. What conditions of love are centered on the qualities that create a lasting love?

5. Can any problems actually be solved by an extramarital affair? Wouldn't this add to existing complications?

Multicolored Love

You're sitting in the park when you notice a handsome thirty-something black man and his family. His wife is an attractive redhead with a tan that gives her a beige color. It's immediately obvious to you that she's not black. They have two kids. The older child is about three. That child is busy holding on to a bunch of colorful balloons that are trying to get away from him in the wind. The younger child is just learning to walk. She balances carefully with the help of her parents, each holding a hand as she stumbles forward. What runs through your mind when you see that?

Some wouldn't think anything at all when looking at that family, whereas others would have a mixture of emotional responses. Every adult black American has an opinion on interethnic relationships.* That's because this is yet another area in which every move by a black man is preceded by negative stereotypes. Another arena in which the actions, ideas, opinions, and beliefs of one individual are seen to represent all black men. However, just as with many other issues concerning black men, there is a shroud of mythology and emotion surrounding this issue that prevents us from seeing the whole truth.

As a change from what is typically written on this subject, I'm going to present a different view. Instead of delving into things from emotion and the desire to be politically correct,

---

* The author's use of the term "interethnic" to denote relationships between people of different colors and heritages acknowledges that all humanity comprises what is known as the human race while recognizing that there are various ethnicities within the human race that give us distinct and unique differences. For more on this, see a later section of this chapter, "Realize What We Call Interracial Is Really Interethnic Love."

I'm approaching the issue of stereotypes about black men in relationships with nonblack women for what it really is—another set of destructive stereotypes about black men.

Basically there are ten major stereotypes about black men who are dating or married to nonblack women, be they Asian, Mexican, Puerto Rican, Indian, Jewish, Native American, of the various Euroethnic blends we too simply refer to as "white people," or any of the other ethnicities on the face of this earth. These stereotypes can be likened to miniature court cases that go on in the minds of many black people. At a simple glance, black men are charged, tried, and convicted of one or more of the following ten stereotypes:

1. HE DOESN'T LIKE BLACK WOMEN

The implication here is that if a black man is dating or married to a nonblack woman, he must have a preference for women who don't look like him. As if he has somehow turned his back on all black women, saying they aren't beautiful enough or good enough. Underpinning this issue is the belief that he must hate himself and all black people so much that he can't bear to experience love with a black woman.

That's a gigantic assumption. Being involved with a woman from another ethnic group doesn't necessarily mean a black man thinks black women aren't good enough for him or desirable. It most certainly doesn't mean he isn't attracted to black women. A nonblack mate doesn't indicate an overall preference for nonblack women.

However, take, for example, a brother who says he doesn't and won't marry or date black women at all. This man does in fact have a serious problem. He does hate himself and he'd benefit from seeking help. All we can do is pray for him, because he may be headed for a rude awakening. This man doesn't realize that choosing to be involved with a woman of another ethnicity won't erase his blackness or shield him from prejudice. But his warped opinion doesn't represent all or the majority of black men in love with nonblack women.

2. HE MUST HAVE LOST HIS MIND

In terms of black men dating or marrying white women specifically, I hear people saying about black men: "They turned to white women." As if they "turned" to drinking, drugs, or alcohol. But that isn't usually the case. Most black men involved with nonblack women haven't gone insane.

At the bottom of this stereotype is the belief that the media and society as a whole have taken hold of the black man's mind and purged it of any thought that black women can be beautiful. As a result, the poor brainwashed black man loses control of his mind and is unconsciously drawn to all women who are anything other than black. While it is true that the American standard of beauty is based largely upon a likeness to whiteness, that is not a logical or realistic reason to explain why some black men have dated or married nonblack women. Dr. Earl Hutchinson commented on this stereotype in his book *Beyond O.J.: Race, Sex and Class Lessons for America*. "Much of this boils down to opinion, gossip, anecdote, rumor, envy, jealousy and ignorance. There is no evidence that black men and white women who date or marry are psychologically impaired."

On the other hand, black women are generally given the benefit of the doubt when they date or marry nonblack men. Sisters will say, "She had to do what she had to do." "I can understand why she had to go and do that." Or they'll say, "She just wanted to be treated right." We can infer from all those statements that there is something wrong with black men. Therefore, because of the lack of good choices, those black women had to look elsewhere. That is an unfair double standard.

The truth is that a person isn't somehow pushed into a decision to date or marry someone from another ethnic group. It's something that occurs naturally in a society full of men and women of varying ethnicities. As Dr. Audrey Chapman says in her book *Entitled to Good Loving,* "Despite the dynamics at play in interracial relationships, most interracial couples do not intentionally set out to find someone of another race, but happen to meet their partner through working together, living in the same apartment building, belonging to the same gym, and other casual encounters. They are usually drawn to each other because of personal traits that may have little to do with race."

3. SUCCESSFUL BLACK MEN ALWAYS SEEK NONBLACK WOMEN

This is another misconception. The vast majority (the key word being "majority") of black athletes, professionals, business executives, entrepreneurs, and entertainers date and marry black women. Perhaps, as a group, a larger number of them have married women of other ethnicities. But not the majority of them. Only a small percentage. When assessing this we have to realize that everything high-profile black men do takes place in a fishbowl. Every action is analyzed and scrutinized. Too many people assume that what one black man does all black men do. But that's not the case.

4. HE HAS FORGOTTEN WHERE HE CAME FROM

While most successful black men are not dating or married to nonblack women, this stereotype is waiting in the wings for those who do. This idea attempts to explain away interethnic

relationships as the case of a black man trying to separate himself from his own blackness. It's also interesting to note that
this stereotype is also applied to other aspects of the black
social system. Blacks who have moved up the professional ladder, relocated to upscale neighborhoods, or attended majority
white schools and universities are often accused and convicted
of not being black enough.

The stereotype that says "he has forgotten where he came
from" unfairly spills over onto black men who have married or
are dating nonblack women. Most of these men aren't attempting to separate themselves from the black community. However, due to the prevalence of this stereotype, some blacks may
see it that way. As a result, these black men who have not in
fact abandoned the black community may find, in some cases,
that members of the black community may abandon them.
While some don't let this hinder their lives, others draw back
from the black community to prevent their mates, families, and
themselves from being the target of mistreatment.

5. HE IS TRYING TO MAKE A SOCIAL STATEMENT

Some black people think that when a black man has a white
girlfriend or wife, it is his way of announcing to the world that
he has "arrived." A way of saying he has overcome the "man"
by getting his woman. Perhaps true for some warped minds.
But not all black men involved with white women are trying to
make a social or political statement.

In fact, most men I've spoken with didn't see things that
way. Rather, they were more concerned about their possible
loss of status due to unfair stereotypes about them held by
blacks and whites alike. Particularly, they had concerns that
other blacks might make a wholesale misinterpretation that
their choice of a white mate indicated a lack of black aware-

ness. But that's the stereotype. In reality it usually isn't the case.

6. EVERY BLACK MAN'S FANTASY IS TO HAVE A NONBLACK WOMAN

There are some black men out there who have the misperception that having a woman who is Asian, Euroethnic, Mexican, or whatever is the answer to some dream. But they are the minority of black men. They obviously have some deep-seated problems if they think a woman of another ethnicity is the answer to their dreams simply because she isn't black.

On the other hand, the black man you see walking through the mall holding his Asian girlfriend's hand doesn't automatically deserve to be placed in that category. What's even more ironic is that this judgment is applied to more than nonblack women. Some black women will get angry if they see a dark-skinned black man, such as myself, with an olive-skinned black woman. I've dated black women who look whiter than the whitest white women. One sister I dated had natural green eyes and long blondish hair. Of course, I was then tried and convicted of being color-struck. Where does all this madness end?

7. HE JUST CAN'T HANDLE A SISTER

This is the belief that black men get involved with women of other colors because they aren't capable of handling the spunk of black women. We have to be careful here, because this stereotype buys into old sexual myths about black women. In particular the Jezebel and Sapphire stereotypes. The belief that every black woman is spunky, funky, and sexually insatiable. Of course, that's not true. Many black women are conservative and quiet. And they don't roll their eyes and jerk their necks in circles.

But it is this idea of a man "handling a sister" that leads to the stereotype. It is the belief that when you see a mixed-ethnic couple, the black man is too weak for his own kind and the woman he is with will cater to his weaknesses. Not only is this unfair, it's insulting. I've seen black women and women of all other colors who will put up with anything and everything men dish out. That's a woman issue, not a color issue.

8. HE'S MAKING THE AFRICAN AMERICAN MALE SHORTAGE WORSE

I've heard this question many times. "Why go outside of your ethnic group when there's so many available black women?" On the surface, that's a valid point. But only if you consider a relationship something that is supposed to happen by planning and design based on physical characteristics.

If you believe love is a response to a higher call, you can't look at it as something that you can design like clothing that you slip into. It's not as though every black woman in the world lines up in front of every black man and offers herself to him. And even if that happened, rising in love isn't just about people being the right height, color, weight, and having the right kind of job. For it to last, lovers have to get the right energy from each other. That's about many factors. If color were the most important ingredient in making relationships work, America wouldn't have a divorce rate that's around 50 percent.

9. IT'S JUST JUNGLE FEVER

Many of us have dined at the sexual buffet table. "I'll take one of those. I'll have some of that. A little dollop of that one would be nice . . ." One doesn't have to cross ethnic lines to have done that. But when black men and white women are involved, the notion of jungle fever is brought in. The belief that black men and white women come together more out of curiosity than anything else. True enough, there is lots of curiosity out there and many black men and white women move to satisfy that curiosity.

But as with all the other stereotypes, that isn't the whole story. Curiosity is one thing. Being in love is another. Thinking that other people could be involved with us only out of curiosity directly supports another stereotype about ourselves. The notion that black men are only sexual objects and not sensual beings. Black men are beautiful creations and any woman can find a black man attractive physically, mentally, and spiritually. It doesn't always have to be jungle fever.

10. HE WON'T TEACH HIS BIRACIAL CHILDREN ABOUT BLACK CULTURE

There's concern that biracial children will forget their black heritage as they grow up. Unfortunately this country still makes people "choose" an ethnicity when they are a mixture of cultures. But many people of mixed heritage are now asserting their right to be biracial. It's a topic of discussion for the next census.

An example of this is the young golfer legend Tiger Woods. There are some blacks who are angry that he doesn't come out and claim he's black. But Tiger has two heritages and he can't be expected to say he is only black, because he's not. His father is black and his mother is Thai. How can he love one side of himself more than the other? This thinking is the residue of the old "one-drop rule." The rule that said one drop of black blood made you black. But today we're entering a time when people are demanding their right to really be who they are, not just one side of themselves or who society wants them to be.

Biracial kids should learn both of their cultures and rejoice in them. Some households celebrate Kwanzaa and Hanukkah. Some people go to a mosque with their fathers and a sanctified Baptist church with their mothers. If your father is from India and your mother is a black woman from Chicago, you have both of those heritages to draw upon. In fact, if we look closely, there are hardly any Americans who are pure anything. I know my family tree has a variety.

HOW WE CAN HEAL THESE STEREOTYPES

In an interview with *Essence* magazine, Whoopi Goldberg used the term "cultural police" to describe people who try to determine who and what is black enough. What we often do to ourselves is discourage each other from daring to think anything off the politically correct path. But rather than do that, we should be tolerant of different ideas and learn whatever can be learned from them. At the very least, we should agree to disagree in a civil manner.

That's why instead of agreeing with these and all the other stereotypes about black men in this book, we need to heal them. Otherwise they threaten to further fragment the black community. There are five things we can do to erase these negative stereotypes: (1) Realize that what we call interracial is really interethnic love. (2) Realize that we all live in one small world. (3) Focus on the big picture. (4) Realize that black is beautiful. (5) Realize that marriage to a nonblack person is not a divorce from blackness.

REALIZE WHAT WE CALL INTERRACIAL IS REALLY INTERETHNIC LOVE

God created only one race of earthlings: humans. Racial-purity arguments are dangerous because that has been the agenda of so many ruthless figures throughout history who have attempted genocide. The human race is the race. It may be hard for some to accept, but we are all one human family belonging to God the Father and Mother Earth. We're dealing with the topic of interethnic relationships within the same human family, not interracial. An interracial relationship would be that of a human being and a Martian. And even in that case, both are God's creations.

ONE SMALL WORLD

Whether we like it or not, the world is getting smaller. For example, a friend and I had a blast one afternoon on the Internet by accessing a Web site that allowed us to browse through personal ads from women all over the world. Innovations in transportation technology are shortening the time of airplane flights around the world. In the foreseeable future, we'll have international colonies living in space. One result of all that will be more and more men and women of different ethnicities falling in love. But that's all right, because, as we move into a new millennium, we're going to have to focus more on humanity and less on colors and ethnicities anyway. Otherwise the entire human race will be nothing more than a memory. Unfortunately our cultural and spiritual development hasn't kept pace with our technology.

THE BIG PICTURE

Consider what humanity is facing at this hour: global warming, melting polar ice caps, prophecies of the apocalypse, a delicate world economy, cloning, gigantic meteors aiming at the earth, holes growing in the ozone, UFOs, world overpopulation, nations in the Third World lacking enough food and drinkable water, and the emergence of killer viruses that medical technology can't defeat. Those are just a few of the problems that at this very moment threaten to wipe out the human race. With so many real problems to solve, is the idea of men and women of different ethnic groups dating and marrying one of the most important things to concern ourselves with?

BLACK IS BEAUTIFUL

The svelte and sexy Tyra Banks snagged a place on the coveted cover of the 1997 *Sports Illustrated* Swimsuit Edition. She is the first black woman ever to have accomplished that. I can say with certainty that there are lots of nonblack men who would love to have a date with Tyra. Handsome and dashing Denzel Washington was named sexiest man alive by *People* magazine last year. Denzel is married. But don't you know that women of every color under the sun would be chasing him if he weren't?

Folks, that's not affirmative action, that's sex appeal. It's a universal language. Other people find us attractive. That's not an attack on our unity, it's just human reality. And the fact of the matter is, we also find other ethnic groups attractive. It's nothing new. Finding other human beings attractive is natural.

MARRYING A NONBLACK ISN'T A DIVORCE FROM BEING BLACK

People who try to forget that they are black don't have to marry outside the black community to do that. A person who is married to a black person can still be doing all kinds of things to destroy the black community. For example, is a black drug dealer married to a black woman a credit to the black community?

The idea of being a traitor to the black community is something that should be based on a person's actions, not simply whom they marry. Consider the achievements of the following influential blacks. Nobody who knows black history could use the word "traitor" to describe any of them. These four individuals made contributions not only to black history but to the entire nation.

THURGOOD MARSHALL

Many people know Thurgood Marshall only as the first African American to sit on the U.S. Supreme Court. But long before that Thurgood Marshall had earned the title of "Mr. Civil Rights." In his outstanding career as a lawyer, he successfully argued twenty-nine of thirty-two cases before the Supreme Court. His most remembered legal achievement is probably the victory in *Brown* v. *Board of Education,* which he argued before the Supreme Court. His victory in that case desegregated the schools of the nation. Marshall's second wife was a Hawaiian woman of Filipino heritage. But no one can question his commitment to black America. The record speaks for itself.

MAYA ANGELOU

Maya Angelou is an icon of American literature. Her prolific life spans from her career in show business to work in film and television to her days in the civil rights battle as Northern Coordinator for the Southern Christian Leadership Conference, a position she was requested to take by Dr. Martin Luther King, Jr. Not enough can be said about her powerful and eloquent poetry. It rings with not only a love of black people but a love of all humanity. Angelou's first husband was Greek. But this had no bearing on her demonstrable love and appreciation for black men. For example, while many female leaders criticized the Million Man March, Angelou was there as one of the major featured speakers. She is yet another example of how one doesn't automatically suffer cultural amnesia when you marry outside the black culture.

FREDERICK DOUGLASS

When Frederick Douglass escaped slavery he didn't forget about his brothers and sisters who were still in bondage. Rather than being content with his freedom, Douglass felt a burning passion to liberate his people. During his dynamic life, he started his own newspaper and became an enormously powerful figure in the movement to abolish slavery. He was also critical in the creation of the first black regiment to fight for the Union Army in the Civil War. Douglass was also known to be a staunch advocate for the rights of women. His second wife was white. But as you can see, his loyalty to his people was unquestionable.

CHARLAYNE HUNTER-GAULT

Journalist Charlayne Hunter-Gault is a more contemporary example. Most know her from her impressive career as a journalist on the *MacNeil/Lehrer Newshour*. But she is also a civil rights soldier. She was one of the two blacks who desegregated the University of Georgia at Athens. This literally put her on the firing line in the tumult of the civil rights movement. When she showed up to register, white students rocked her car. Only a couple of nights later, a large group of white students rioted outside her dormitory to protest her presence. But still, Hunter-Gault persevered through it all. Despite the racially charged environment, Hunter-Gault eventually married one of the white students she met at the University of Georgia. But this doesn't lessen the significance of her desegregating the campus. She bravely cleared the way for others.

The names could go on and on: outspoken basketball superstar Charles Barkley, Oscar-winning actor Cuba Gooding, Jr., supermodel Iman, celebrated actor James Earl Jones, entertainment entrepreneur Quincy Jones, groundbreaking actor Sidney Poitier, soul diva Diana Ross, and acclaimed novelist Alice Walker. But these names are sufficient to make the point. Marriage to a nonblack person isn't a divorce from being black.

The truth of the matter is that to truly love anyone, regardless of whether their skin matches ours or not, we have to get beyond mere physical definitions. When we put physical and material boundaries on love we lessen its potency. Love is the essence of our very souls. A euphoric awareness and consciousness beyond what we can see and touch. It is a human model of our relationship with the creator. All this doesn't come in the nice neat package we always think it should. Love comes as it comes. It's up to us whether we accept it.

Think about it.

THINGS TO THINK ABOUT

1. Since skin color is only a physical characteristic, should it be such a dominant factor in selecting a soul mate?

2. Given that prejudice exists, do you believe inter-ethnic relationships are more difficult? Or, as in any other relationship, does the ultimate success of inter-ethnic relationships depend upon how two individuals approach the challenges they face as a couple?

3. Have you ever found yourself stereotyping black men who are in relationships with nonblack women or black women who are in relationships with nonblack men? What are your thoughts? How can you grow beyond those stereotypes?

The Ten Things Women Do That Drive Men Away

Some women, without even knowing it, are driving the men who love them right out of their lives. For the most part, women aren't getting information about men straight from the source. They're asking other women, listening to so-called relationship experts, and believing statistics. While those sources may be helpful and provide some information, nothing is as accurate as asking men what they think and feel. This list of ten things women do that drive men away was compiled from informal interviews with real everyday men. None of these men are "experts" from academia. None of them are sociologists, psychologists, or relationship experts. They're just regular guys: a computer technician, a personal fitness trainer, a mail courier, a college student, an entrepreneur, a corporate executive, a sanitation worker, a police officer, a mechanic, and an attorney.

When I got the guys together, the first question I asked was "What are some of the things women do that drive men away?" I asked them to be blunt and candid in their responses, but I made it clear that I wasn't looking for a list of meanspirited complaints. Instead, I wanted to compile a list of ten things that men wished women knew. A list that would bridge the gap between men and women. I told them the purpose of this list was to improve communication, avoid misunderstanding, and expose any "taboo" issues that need to be brought into the open. In that spirit, we began our discussion. As I sat and talked with the guys, most of their answers kept coming back to the ten areas explained below.

1. ACTING SWEET TO GET A MAN, THEN CHANGING

"I don't know why women act so sweet during dating and change completely when they know they've got you." —Alvin, computer technician

She used to go to bed in a naughty nightie and didn't care about sweating the curls out of her head. Now she goes to bed with a head full of rollers and a face covered with Noxzema. When they were dating, she batted her eyes, spoke softly, and always looked sexy. But now that she's got him, that all changed. The gently batting eyes and shy smiles have been replaced with frowns, pursed lips, and shrill tones. No more sexy clothes. Now she dresses like she doesn't care what she looks like, every day is a bad hair day, and she's fast losing the curves in her body and developing a pleasantly plump figure.

Of course, men can't expect women to be superwomen who are able to work, cook, clean, and make love with flawless precision. But a woman shouldn't start out playing the superwoman role at the beginning and then change. It's better to present herself as she is and get it all out in the open. When a woman changes her entire act after the relationship gets going, men feel as though they've been duped. Suddenly, he doesn't know what to believe anymore and feels he can't really trust the woman he thought he knew.

2. NOT GIVING ENOUGH SPACE

"She clings to me because she thinks that every minute I'm not with her I'm fooling around." —Lewis, personal fitness trainer

The "S" word must be used carefully. Some men intentionally abuse the term "I need my space" to ensure that they can have their cake and eat it too—fool around while not giving up what they already have. But not all men are that way. Most men simply just want some room to be by themselves. Men, just like women, need to feel that they aren't trapped or being held hostage in their lives. From time to time, men want to get away and be alone or hang out with their friends.

But it's a strain on the relationship when women think that a man is being selfish, silly, or making up an excuse to go out and cheat just because he wants some space. The smart woman knows that a man needs his space and doesn't hold it against him. She's confident enough to know that each person needs his/her own space to maintain a healthy relationship. On the other hand, jealous and possessive women are well known for their deliberate attempts to prevent a man from having any sort of privacy. Those are the women who think letting a man out of their sight is a mistake. They keep choke holds on their men and eventually drive them away. But if a woman can't give the man a little space, either the relationship isn't solid or she has some personal problems she needs to deal with. If it's because she can't trust him out of her sight, she doesn't need that man anyway.

3. WANTING TOO MANY THINGS

"I'm just a working man. I can't afford a two-story house in the suburbs, a Lexus, a Range Rover, a bunch of credit cards, and kids too." —Jesse, mail courier

Some black men say black women are unrealistic in their expectations and want too much. Of course, wanting a good hardworking man who respects women isn't asking too much. But what about when it goes far beyond that? For some women, having a good man just isn't enough. They also want a Lexus, a two-story home in the suburbs, and a string of credit cards. When they don't have these things, they moan and complain as though life is terrible. If the man dares to say something about how he's happy with things as they are, he'll be accused of being complacent, lazy, and lacking ambition. It's fine to have goals and want some luxuries. But counting the blessings you already have never hurts either.

4. NOT SAYING WHAT SHE MEANS

"Women expect you to read their minds like a psychic."
—Jamal, college student

Men aren't very good mind readers. In fact, we often have difficulty just figuring out what women mean with the words they speak. I think women are far more sophisticated communicators than men; they seem to be more adept at the subtleties of gestures, facial expressions, and body language. Therefore, men and women almost always suffer from communication breakdowns in relationships.

Unfortunately, some women do not express themselves honestly and openly. It seems that they are more apt to use voice inflections and body language to communicate what they mean, even when the actual words they are saying convey the opposite. Take this situation, for example: "No, I don't mind if you go out with your friends instead of taking me to a movie tonight," a woman says, tapping her foot and looking away with her arms folded. Although her mouth is saying quite literally, "No, I don't mind," her body is saying she does mind. Women expect the men in their lives to read their nonverbal cues.

Some men fail to read the nonverbal cues of the women in their lives. When this happens, an argument is almost always the result, because the woman feels that she communicated her feelings to the man and he ignored her. For example, I'll use the scenario from the previous paragraph. When that man comes home from his night out with the guys, his wife is going to be angry at him. She'll probably snap at him when she talks, slam doors, or even yell at him.

"What's the problem?" he'll ask.

"You know what the problem is!"

But he really may not know what the problem is, because she never came out and said what she meant in words. She expected him to read the nonverbal cues and he totally missed them. As a result, the woman believes that the man is just being callous and self-centered. Likewise, the man is upset too; he thinks she's nagging him for no reason. Both of them will go to bed angry.

5. THE THREE B'S OF SEX

"I'm going to be straight about it: sex is important to me."
—Gene, entrepreneur

Perhaps it would be nice if sex didn't play such a major role in relationships. But for most people, sex is a big part of a relationship. And for men, it's probably more important than it should be. The sexual aggravations of men boil down to the three B's: bad, boring, and the boudoir battle.

Bad sex

Sex is a learned skill. It's similar to driving a car. Basically, anyone can do it. Some are good at it. And others are experts. But everyone has an idea of what they consider good and bad sex. Common complaints among men are: lack of enthusiasm, lack of rhythm, no creativity, and poor technique. If a person in a relationship is dissatisfied or experiencing sexual dysfunction, it's something that should be openly and honestly discussed. The reasons for sexual dysfunction can be psychological, physiological, ethical, and religious, or a host of other things. If the problems seem insurmountable, the advice of a pastor or therapist may be necessary.

Boring sex

Boring sex isn't necessarily the same thing as bad sex. But it is far from good. Boring sex is always doing it in the same place, at the same time, and in the same old position. It's when the sex gets to the point that it feels like more of a duty than a desire. Boring sex is when you're going through all the motions but there's no spice or passion involved.

Boudoir battle

Using sex as a weapon doesn't do anything but make a man angry. It can be subtle things such as not being open to touching and cuddling. Or it can be more strategic. It can be the refusal to do certain things in bed. The most brutal form of bedroom battle is outright refusal.

Of course, a man can't expect a woman who is angry at him to make mad, passionate love to him. That's where communication comes into play. It's far better to talk and resolve the differences than to play games of will because any real man will be very insulted by such behavior. Then he may become vengeful and the whole thing turns into a cold war of revenge. Boudoir battle can lead to deep resentment and some men will use it as an excuse to cheat on their wives or girlfriends.

6. CONSTANTLY TALKING ABOUT OTHER MEN

"She's always talking about this guy at her job and it really pisses me off." —Shawn, corporate executive

Men don't like to hear women constantly talking about other men. It's not necessarily an ego thing. It's just that each man wants to feel special and important to the woman in his life.

Women don't have to cradle us like babies. Nor do they need to be patronizing. But a woman would be wise to realize that the ego of a man can be fragile. Black men in particular are constantly attempting to gain and maintain the basic elements of American manhood: the ability to provide, protect, and be masters of our own destinies. Not talking excessively to your husband or boyfriend about how great you think other men are is one small thing that can go a long way toward healing the beleaguered black male ego.

7. BEING A DRAMA QUEEN

"She calls my pager all day when I'm at work. Then when I call her back, she just starts whining about some little thing that could've waited until later." —Art, sanitation worker

Drama queens are always whining, pestering, or nagging about something. With them, nothing can ever be right. They pull all kinds of little tricks to get and control a man's attention. If he's watching television, she wants him to get up and put out the trash. When he has time off from work, she tries to plan each hour for him. If it's bill-paying time, she's crying about her car note being late.

Another technique used by the drama queen is to play damsel in distress to get a man's attention. In this role the drama queen says "save me." Initially, it may make a man feel good to be the chivalrous knight in shining armor coming to the rescue. But too much distress can drive even the most loyal knight to ride off into the sunset.

8. BEING HARD AND COLD

"I work the graveyard shift so I don't have to be at home with my wife." —Derek, police officer

That response was from a man who had been married less

than one year and was already engaged in a cold war with his wife. Most of the time she was openly disrespectful to him as a human being, not just as a man. Other times she was cold and aloof, barely acknowledging that he was in the room. Believe it or not, men have feelings too. Hard and cold behavior is enough to drive anyone away. Again, we aren't asking to be cradled like babies. But every man wants home to be a safe refuge from the coldhearted world. However, when the world at home is colder than the work world, there is no solace.

9. CHEATING

"They call us dogs, but women are out there fooling around just as much." —Barry, auto mechanic

Some women will maintain that when a woman is cheating it's always the fault of a man. That simply isn't true. Women are human beings and are therefore just as subject to dishonesty and deceit as any man.

Cheating takes two forms. First, there's the obvious form, which is having affairs. But the second way of cheating is mental. It's the subtle art of getting over on him. She may not be fooling around with another man but she may be cheating by fooling around with the checkbook balance. Her body may be faithful, but she may be cheating by playing manipulative games to keep him within her control. Such games rob a man of his energy and creativity and prevent him from realizing his full potential. The truth is that cheating doesn't have to be just about affairs or lovers. Cheating is deception of any kind.

10. ENGAGING IN A POWER STRUGGLE

"I can't stand it when a woman always wants to prove to me that she's smart, tough, and independent." —Lawrence, attorney

It really irritates men when women they're involved with are constantly trying to upstage them. This is especially bothersome for those men who aren't trying to compete with their mates. This behavior takes many forms. Some women who engage in power struggles with their mates do it through career competition: who can make the most money or get the most prestige? For some the competition is based upon education level: who has the most advanced degree from the most prestigious school? Another form of engaging in a power struggle is competing in disagreements: who gets the last word in? In addition to those power struggles, the men I spoke with mentioned four other ways some women engage in a power struggle: (1) Making sure they look smarter than a man by intentionally upstaging him in public. (2) Disagreeing for the sake of disagreement. (3) Unnecessary rudeness. (4) Being condescending or cutting down what a man says when he states his personal thoughts and opinions.

The guys I spent the evening talking with agreed that they weren't intimidated by women who made more money, drove more expensive cars, or had more education than they did. Their issue was with women who want to flaunt those things in order to be the superior person in a relationship. They all agreed that such behavior was a complete turnoff. No matter what form the power struggle comes in, it's an energy drain for a man who isn't interested in competing with his mate. Engaging in a power struggle is a quick way to drive a man away.

––––––

I know this list is going to make the tempers of some women flare. But remember, this isn't a list of complaints. It's information intended to give women insight into what men are thinking; it's a bridge across the communication gap. Without straight and candid communication, we can't solve the issues that threaten to end so many relationships. Use these ten issues as a starting point for a dialogue with your husband, the man in your life, or a male friend. Such a discussion will give you even better insight than reading this list. And that's the one-on-one communication needed not only to save relationships but to make them better.

THINGS TO THINK ABOUT

1. Do you know any women who act sweet to get a man and then change after they've got him? Why do you think they do that?

2. What can women who feel uncomfortable about their men wanting space and time alone do to assure themselves that his time alone is a good thing for their relationship?

3. Have you and your significant other come to an agreement on what expenses are acceptable and necessary within your relationship? If married, have you and your husband come to an agreement on what your necessary expenses are? Have you constructed a plan to achieve your financial goals as a couple?

4. Do you communicate directly with your significant other or do you expect him to read your nonverbal cues?

5. Have you and your significant other discussed how mutual sexual satisfaction can be achieved within your relationship?

6. Are you careful not to talk about other men in the presence of your significant other in a manner that makes him feel berated?

7. Are you a drama queen?

8. What things can you do to make time with your man something he looks forward to for soothing his mind, body, and soul?

9. What motivates a woman who cheats? What are some ways (other than sexual) in which some women cheat in relationships?

10. What can you and your significant other do to keep your lives from becoming sources of power struggles?

Old Baggage Kills New Love

Rob was high with excitement. It had only been a month but he felt that what he and Sherry had was the best love of his life. Tuesday, he spent almost the entire day at work on the phone with her, whispering details of their secret rendezvous. The next morning both of them were going to call in sick. Little did their bosses know that those calls would actually come from a beach where Rob and Sherry were snuggled in a hotel suite. Rob's bags were packed and he was heading to Sherry's apartment after work. From there they were going straight to the beach.

Rob worked late to finish a report his supervisor needed for the monthly meeting the next morning. It was after dark when he left the office. Halfway to Sherry's apartment, Rob realized that he hadn't left an important memo on his boss's desk that also had to be there the next morning. If the memo wasn't there, his absence would be very noticeable. Rob hooked his black Acura around in the middle of the road and zipped back to the office. He quickly typed the short memo. He also skimmed his report again and found a small mistake. He corrected the mistake and left all the paperwork on his boss's desk. He was now forty-five minutes late.

He got back on the freeway and was immediately ensnared in stalled traffic caused by a big accident a mile up the road. He was going to be very late. He reached into the glove compartment for his mobile phone. It wasn't there. It was still in the drawer at his office. With no other solution at hand, he had to accept that he was going to be even later than he already was. Rob inched along until he passed the accident scene almost an hour later. Then the pace quickly shot back to normal. By now he was a total of an hour and a half late.

Rob trotted up the stairs to the second level. He was already full of tension from working late. A romantic dinner and sunset on the bay was going to be the perfect cure for his stress. He paused at the door to think of something funny to say about being late. Sherry loved his offbeat sense of humor. Then he knocked.

Sherry ripped the door open. Her eyes were red and puffy. Her mascara was smeared and running down the sides of her face. Suddenly, she disappeared from the doorway into the dark living room. Concerned, Rob began to step forward into the apartment until he felt cold water splash his face. At the same instant he saw a vase fly by his head and a dozen roses hit him in the face. "Take your stupid roses," Sherry screamed. She stormed into her bedroom and came out with a teddy bear. She threw it at him from the door of the bedroom. "Take your stupid teddy bear," she screamed again. Then she ran into the kitchen. She bent to open the refrigerator, turned around, and hurled an apple pie at him. "Here's the apple pie I made for you."

Rob stood there dripping with water. Rose petals stuck to his white shirt, along with apple-pie filling. "You're a drama queen," he yelled. "I thought you had it together. But you're just as insane as my last girlfriend." At that, Sherry slammed the door in his face. Then Rob really got angry. He kicked the door. "It's over, Sherry. We're finished," he said, pounding the door with his fists and kicking it with his right foot. "You're not going to be going off on me for no reason. It's over!"

Rob finally kicked the door so hard that he hurt his foot. He grunted and leaned back against the rail around the courtyard. That's when he noticed three security guards eyeing him. He had to leave or they were going to call the police. He hobbled off on one foot, cursing Sherry as a psycho and vowing never to talk to her again.

Inside the apartment, Sherry watched through the peephole as the security guards escorted Rob off the property. Now she was convinced that all men were cheating, lying philanderers who had no heart.

She sat down on the couch. The teddy bear was on the floor near the door. She'd named him Robby so that she could cuddle up with him every night. What seemed so right just yesterday was now gone in one quick rage. It was over, she thought. She was not going to get into a relationship with another cheating man.

She picked Robby up from the floor and walked to the kitchen. Looking at the little button eyes on his furry brown face, she felt even worse about the argument. For a fleeting moment she wondered if she was wrong about exploding on Rob. No, she thought. He's pulling the same stunts that my last boyfriend did. It's only going to get worse if I don't end it now. "Goodbye Rob," she whispered as she dropped Robby in the trash.

Another new love killed by old baggage.

Let's make one thing clear here. There are two times Rob should've called. The first was when he went back to the office. At that point, he knew he was going to be late. The second was after he cleared the big traffic jam when he was already late. Rob should've stopped and called from a pay phone. Men, myself included, are notorious for not calling when we're going to be late. We figure we're en route to you anyway. We're coming. So why call? It's the same reason we don't ask for directions. We're going to find our destination anyway. So why waste time stopping and asking? I know it doesn't make sense. It's male illogic. But by not calling, Rob reopened an unresolved issue from Sherry's past and helped kill a blossoming relationship.

Sherry assumed that Rob didn't call because he didn't care. She immediately thought he was going to act just like her last boyfriend, who frequently stood her up at public functions and then didn't answer the phone until late at night, with no good excuse for his absence. However, in Rob's case, Sherry shares half the blame as well. Before jumping to a hasty conclusion she should have stopped to consider that Rob might have a good reason for being late. Sherry should have given Rob the benefit of the doubt but instead became hysterical and instantly pressed Rob's buttons and reminded him of his last girlfriend who was an emotionally draining drama queen, she always screamed and yelled at Rob when the slightest thing upset her. Her behavior was so exhausting that Rob vowed he'd never go through anything like it again, not even with Sherry.

Now it's over. No happy storybook ending. Just hard feelings.

Old emotional baggage is what's left after the breakup of a relationship. It's composed of all the worst things you remember about a person and the way you were treated by them. The memories left by old emotional baggage will change the way you view future relationships. But the results of old baggage don't have to change your views of future relationships in a negative way. Positive results come from old baggage when we change our behavior in ways that will prevent us from making the mistakes we've made in the past.

However, if we don't make positive changes from old emotional baggage, it can make us bitter. Then we'll undoubtedly take out our frustrations on men and women we meet in the future, sabotaging our chances for fulfilling relationships. That's what happened to Rob and Sherry. Both Rob and Sherry probably could easily have worked it out with some communication. But they didn't even get to talk because they both exploded on the basis of their past issues.

Here's what Rob and Sherry could've done differently.

How to Handle Emotional Baggage

1. At the beginning of a relationship, you and your significant other should discuss the emotional-baggage issues that each of you have. Discussing these issues at the beginning of a relationship can help prevent potentially explosive misunderstandings. Or if a big argument is provoked by an issue, at least your significant other has an idea as to why you're angry.
2. If an emotional-baggage issue does arise, don't blow your top! Remain calm. Close your eyes and count slowly to ten. Meditate quietly for a moment. Or take some deep breaths. Relax before you say anything.
3. Say to yourself, "What he/she just did brings back some bad memories for me. But this is not my previous relationship. This is another person. I owe him/her the benefit of the doubt."
4. After you've cooled down, let your significant other know what he/she did to trigger a painful issue for you. Discuss it with him/her.
5. Apologize if you blew your top. Ask him/her to be patient and to continue working through it with you.

For more discussion on emotional baggage, see the chapter "How to Recover from a Broken Heart."

EMOTIONAL-BAGGAGE ASSESSMENT

In the exercise below, fill in the names of five people you've had relationships with or dated who left you saying, "I'll never put up with that again." Add more names if you need to. You should also include people you've had other types of relationships with, such as your mother, father, brother, sister, a friend, etc. They are also sources of emotional baggage that many people take into relationships. Then identify the issue you struggled over and what emotional baggage you were left with. For example:

MY EMOTIONAL BAGGAGE

NAME	ISSUE	BAGGAGE
Zack	tried to control and manipulate me	sensitive to men giving me advice or making too many suggestions about what I should do; makes me feel as though they're trying to control me

NAME	ISSUE	BAGGAGE
1.		
2.		
3.		
4.		
5.		

POINTS TO REMEMBER

- Broken relationships leave us with emotional baggage.
- Every man and woman should know his/her emotional baggage.
- Unresolved emotional baggage can ruin new relationships.
- You and your significant other should discuss the emotional baggage each of you have and be sensitive to the issues of the other. You can work through the issues together if both of you know what they are.
- Emotional baggage can also come from other sources in our lives, such as family, friends, acquaintances, and business associates.

You Can't Change Him

Ladies, one of the hardest things about love is accepting the fact that the man you ultimately fall in love with most likely won't fulfill your fantasy. He'll be more reality than fantasy, more fact than fiction. Instead of a smile like Denzel's, he may have a couple of crooked teeth. Instead of having a super-jock body, he may be a few pounds overweight. Instead of dressing like a *GQ* cover model, he may prefer wearing jeans and a T-shirt. Instead of being rich and famous, he may be a hardworking blue-collar brother.

Lots of women would do themselves a big favor by giving up the idea of trying to reshape, remodel, and "make men over." Women should learn to accept men at face value. This desire to "train a man" seems to spring from the idea that some women truly believe men don't know what's good for them. This type of woman acts as though all men are aimlessly stumbling around in a dark, cold void. She feels that men only start living when they meet her. She thinks that only she has the power to deliver men from their drab lives and transform them into something greater. Or, more aptly stated, what *she* thinks is best. Her intent is to change a man's career, beliefs, wardrobe, education, mannerisms, etc.

I don't know if the basis of this thinking is a well-intentioned maternal instinct or the compulsion of a control freak. The "man trainers" may have very good intentions when they attempt to change men, but they usually forget to do one thing. They don't ask the man if he wants to change his ways. Instead, they take off full throttle with a secret strategy to change him. It's usually a very elaborate scheme involving a mixture of tricks she's picked up from friends, sisters, mothers, aunts, and through her own experience. Though the methods vary, most of these strategies include highly advanced mind games, preparing mouthwatering meals, giving thoughtful gifts, and the use of sex as a distraction and brainwashing technique. However, the forced changes probably won't last for very long. When it all blows up in her face, she'll go crying to a talk-show host about how she was used. When actually she played herself.

Why don't man-training projects work? The following scenarios give a few clues.

WILD MONKEYS

The man trainer is constantly searching for a cute little wild monkey that is wandering around lost in the romantic jungle. She wants to take him home, feed him, and clean him up. She believes he'll make a great pet. Her mission with this man is to shave off his rough edges and turn him into a polished socialite with fine clothes and discriminating tastes. She wants to replace his jeans and high-top tennis shoes with expensive loafers and stylish garments with designer labels. She wants to replace his habit of watching football on Sunday afternoon with trips to the museum. She wants to replace his Burger King habit with French, Thai, and Ethiopian cuisine. While she's telling him she loves everything about him, she's thumbing through the pages of *International Male* selecting his new wardrobe. She's working within a time frame that will have him ready for presentation at her next major party or function.

Finally, she wins the first battle and convinces him to stack up some high fashions on his credit card. She's eager to show her friends how well she has dressed her pet. He escorts her to a party given by a friend. She beams with pride and names the designers her monkey is wearing as she parades him around the room. The jeans, high-tops, and T-shirts are gone. He has been transformed into a Chocolate Ken Doll straight from the pages of a fashion magazine. But he looks about as graceful and comfortable as a woman in heels for the first time.

Finally, he escapes outside onto the patio alone. He loosens his collar and removes his painful shoes. He fights an urge to strip the clothes off and run. *I wonder what the score is in the big game,* he thinks. He doesn't like these clothes, the party, the people, and he feels like a monkey all dressed up for a circus act. Feelings of resentment and alienation start creeping into his mind. He won't be around long after that. As far as he's concerned she can have her friends, designer clothes, parties, and find herself another chump. If a man doesn't feel comfortable dressing like a model and being a socialite, you can't make him do it.

MARRIED TO HIS WORK

This is an ironic project because the very thing that attracted the man trainer to this man is the thing that she will ultimately compete with for his attention. In the beginning, she was impressed with his success. She admired how he was always busy wheeling and dealing. But after a few months of marriage nothing has changed. He talks on the cellular phone during the drive home from dinner. Someone's always paging him for something important. Instead of snuggling in the bed, he sits up and hammers away on a laptop computer half the night. In the beginning, she thought that he would stop working so much and start spending more time with her after they were married. But it hasn't happened.

Since nothing has changed, she decides that she must change

him. Her strategy is to compete with his career for attention. She'll try anything from hot-pink lace to spontaneous arguments to divert his attention to her. More often than not, such manipulation will end in a clash. He will start to resent her and then begin to avoid her. In the beginning, his career was the most important thing in the world to him and nothing has changed. In all probability, it will continue to be that way. He's married to his work. That's something she should've carefully and realistically assessed in the beginning. If a man loves his job more than you, you can't change him.

TURNING BAD BOYS INTO GOOD MEN

The transformation of a bad boy into a good man seems to be an ego thing with women who fall into this category. No matter how many times she catches him cheating, she overlooks it. No matter how many times he goes to jail, she bails him out. No matter how many times he promises to get into a drug rehabilitation program, she doesn't put her foot down. Instead of moving on, she becomes more resolved in her attempt to change him. It's as though it's a supreme victory for her if she can tame a wild man and put him on a leash.

Typically, she may allow him to move in without paying half the rent. She views this as a way to clamp down on him and monitor him more closely. But this kind of man probably doesn't have a job, so that fits perfectly into his plan. He's the kind of man who makes excuses to avoid working, borrows the car, uses the gas and then doesn't refill the tank, and comes back with alcohol on his breath and lipstick on his collar.

But she continues to try to change him. She adjusts her strategy. Perhaps she goes from passive to aggressive. Friends and family warn her, but she tunes them out. *They just don't understand him like I do,* she thinks. *If I keep loving him, he'll change,* she believes. But this type of man will continue to take as long as she gives. He's an extraordinarily talented con man who's found a good sucker. He'll keep taking and take her right down into the gutter with him if she doesn't wake up in time. She can't change that.

THE ABUSIVE MAN

Last, there's the most dangerous man-training project: the abusive man. He is a training project taken on by the woman who thinks she will change him and he will eventually stop. Statistically, she's dead wrong. Most abuse escalates in a continuous loop. After every abusive episode there's a cooling-down period, reconciliation, and then another abusive episode worse than the previous incident. A woman involved in this cycle should be warned that she can't change this man. He needs help. Everyone has arguments. But when the loud yelling moves to shoving and the shoving moves to punches and the punches move to kicks and choking, it's time for a quick exit and professional help (i.e., the police and counseling).

Unfortunately, I've listened to some women tell stories of abuse with what actually seemed to be a glow of pride. They tell how their man knocked them out cold or slapped them across the face so hard they smashed into a wall. Believe it or not, there are women who feel such abuse is a display of love by their men, thinking: *He wouldn't get so angry if he didn't love me.* Even more shocking, some women feel that it's a badge of honor to be strong enough to endure abusive relationships. But there are no excuses. If punches and kicks are flying, it's time to go. Hopefully, she will realize this before it comes to a black eye or cracked ribs and before she becomes a crime statistic in a cold morgue. He needs help, and you can't change him.

———

Ladies, remember, you can't change a man. That's a fact. If a man wants to change, he will. The most you can do is be an influence in that process. In relationships, we have to accept differences in others. Or exercise the option of passing that opportunity by for another one. A man isn't like an animal needing to be trained. A man is a human being with his own unique personality, style, and thoughts. No matter what you do, you can't control him. There's only one thing you can control: yourself and whether or not you'll be in his life.

POINTS TO REMEMBER

- Permanent changes in a man's behavior come only when he seeks to change himself for his own reasons. A woman may be able to influence changes in a man, but she can't actually make him change.
- You can't train a man the way you train an animal.
- Observe a man's behavior in the early stages of knowing him because he is not likely to make great changes in his basic character after starting a relationship with you. Ask yourself: Can I live with him the way he is now?
- It's not your job in life to sacrifice your own happiness attempting to convert bad boys into good men.
- Abusive men need professional help. You can only harm yourself and your children by staying in an abusive situation. For more on abusive men, see the chapter "Domestic Violence: Don't Be a Victim."

You can obtain more information on domestic violence by calling: **The National Domestic Violence Hotline at 1-800-799-SAFE**
Tdd for the hearing impaired: 1-800-787-3224
or on the World Wide Web at:
http://www.inetport.com/~ndvh

Single and Complete

It was the end of what had been a long month. When Linda's boss fell ill, the responsibility of making the biggest and most important sales presentation of the year fell upon her shoulders. Suddenly, Linda was the person the entire firm was counting on to win a giant account from their rival. She worked on the presentation obsessively. It put her nerves on edge and cost her a month's sleep. But she knew that if she could pull this off, a promotion and big raise were guaranteed. Finally, she'd finished. The presentation was over and it had gone better than she could ever have dreamed. But now she'd have to bite her nails for another week, waiting to see if she landed the account.

Linda unlocked the door to her town house and walked into the dark silence. Her nose was greeted by the gentle scent of peach potpourri. Her steps echoed across the Italian marble entry as she passed her orderly dining room with a glass table set for two. Leaning against the island in her finely equipped kitchen, she flipped through her mail.

Finally she plopped down on the couch and sank into its supple leather. She exhaled and found the remote to the stereo on the floor. She tried to relax by tuning in to a love ballad by Luther Vandross. His smooth voice drifted her away into a fantasy. She imagined a big strong man easing up behind her and massaging the kinks out of her muscles. Kneading and squeezing her shoulders, arms, and legs. But it was only a passing thought. She had no man in her life. There hadn't been for a while. Even during her five years of marriage, scenes such as that had rarely occurred. She'd long ago learned to cope with random loneliness. But on this particular Friday night, some male company would've been nice. Having none, she turned out the lights and burned candles. Then she slipped under a sheet of hot water scented with essential oils. She spoiled herself. After all, she deserved it.

A few town houses down the row, John let out a victorious yell with his fists raised in the air. He'd done it. Three years ago people were calling him crazy for leaving his steady job to chase a dream. Today, those same people couldn't believe that his one-man computer repair service had grown into a full-blown business servicing major corporate and governmental clients. He no longer wore all the hats either. Now he had a full-time sales representative, three full-time technicians, a secretary, and he was still growing. But, best of all, today he'd paid off the loan he took to start his business. Now it looked as though it would be smooth sailing in the profitable black ink. He had a good reason to celebrate.

Outside on the patio, he turned a chicken on the grill. He felt a passing loneliness. It would be nice to take a special lady to dinner tonight and toast his success with the bottle of Dom Pérignon he'd bought for the occasion. But there was nobody special in his life. He could get a date. But this was a special moment—a moment to savor with a special person. He decided that special person was himself. John did celebrate that night. Alone on the patio, he feasted on grilled chicken and raised a toast of Dom Pérignon high in the air to himself.

John and Linda are single but complete. They are single people with whole lives. Sometimes they get lonely; that's natural. But their loneliness isn't a desperate void waiting to be filled by someone else. They feel a peculiar type of loneliness felt only by complete singles. It's a tolerable discomfort. John and Linda aren't people who long to marry for financial gain.

They aren't seeking someone to give their lives meaning or excitement. Linda isn't seeking a man to make her feel pretty. She knows she is. John isn't looking for a woman to marvel at how smart he is. He knows he's smart. John isn't a control freak seeking a woman to dominate. He wants to share. Linda isn't looking for a man to pay her bills. She has a well-established career. All they want is somebody to share their lives with, some soul enhancement.

One might say that John and Linda are good people and they deserve good, soul-enhancing mates. One might say that surely life will reward their good deeds and achievements with true love. But that's not guaranteed. We live in an imperfect world with imperfect people in imperfect situations. Our searches for soul mates aren't resolved simply by what we deserve or don't deserve. There's no easy answer to why the Johns and Lindas out there seem to be perpetually single. Relationship dynamics are as variable as the personalities and circumstances in which we all find ourselves. Then there's the factor of timing. At times we're open to inviting someone new into our lives, and at times we're not. Or it could be as simple as not having met the right person. In a world and times as complex as ours, the variables are infinite.

Ironically, John and Linda live only a few doors down from each other. In a fictional love story, the paths of John and Linda would intersect one day. In reality, that situation may or may not happen. Reality number one of being single and complete is cold and bold: *There is no promise that you will ever find perfect love with another person.* It's a bitter fact for the lonesome and lovesick. But the truth is that no other person possesses perfect love, and therefore no one can give it to you. This is not to say that love doesn't exist. But in our world, that four-letter word has been manipulated, twisted, and broken. Just look at the way many people choose a mate. They rattle off lists of conditions for loving someone. "He has to have a house." "She has to make as much money as I do." "He has to be at least six feet tall." "She has to have some ass." Real unconditional love would not know such ridiculous requirements. If we can't give it, we can't expect it. The love you can expect from other people is imperfect. It may be good, but it will hardly be pure.

The second reality of being single and complete is that *we have no control over love*. We can't make love happen when we want and with whom we want. Love doesn't come and go when we please. Love plays by its own rules. Rules we don't understand. Love doesn't care if John and Linda are the most perfect people in the world. Love doesn't care that Linda sometimes feels alone in her pristine town house where she has an elegant glass dining-room table set for two. Love doesn't care that John is a good man who wishes he had a special woman with whom he could share his moments of success. Love doesn't find its way only to those wo do—or don't— deserve it. People often ask why things happen the way they do. Why do people starve? Why do people kill each other? Why is there disease and suffering in the world? Why can't I find true love? Hard questions without easy answers. Those questions serve to illustrate that our fates are not promised. It's very possible that John and Linda could find themselves in healthy relationships onc day. But it's also possible that they could find themselves in terrible relationships. There's no promise or guarantee either way. Life isn't fair, and love sure as hell isn't.

Shakespeare stated the third and most important fact of being single and complete when he wrote the words *To thine own self be true*. We set ourselves up for failure by looking for salvation in other people. When someone lets us down, which is inevitable, we feel betrayed and deceived. How many women have met Mr. Right, were swept off their feet, and are now picking up the pieces without child support? What about the man who met Ms. Right, only to see her love go out the door the day he was laid off from his job?

The only answer to avoiding the pitfalls of love is to love ourselves first. We can give ourselves a greater love than another person can ever give us. It's only when you fill your life with love for yourself that you become a more loving person. When you love yourself, you want others to feel the buoyancy that you feel. You start to care about the homeless, the hungry people half a world away, the environment, saving vanishing species, your neighbor next door, the crying woman on the news . . . You feel a universal connection with everyone and everything around you. Self-love brings about completion. "To thine own self be true." Others may fail you, but make sure you don't fail yourself.

"Completion" is a word that brings to mind thoughts of wholeness, totality, and security. A single person can be complete. Being single isn't physical, it's a state of mind. Many married people are more single than a person living single and complete could ever be. In life we are ultimately on individual paths. That's why the complete singles won't search for a person to fulfill them, save them, or complete their lives. The complete single is only seeking a companion, a soul mate.

But the search for perfect love from other people is a good teacher. As we move in and out of each other's lives, in and out of lust and love, we learn that love with others can be transient. We learn that we should plant seeds of self-love as a priority. Cultivate those seeds with belief in ourselves, trust in ourselves, and respect for ourselves. From self-grown love, a fruit bursting with love for others will grow. Then we will be ready to seek that special soul mate to enhance us. We will have moved beyond petty conditions and shallow ideals. We won't judge people on their looks, money, or status because we won't be seeking those things from them. As complete singles, we'd be searching for soul mates instead of for keys to a car, money, or a sculpted butt.

Perhaps that is why so many of us can't seem to get it right after so many tries. We're asking the wrong questions but getting the right answers. We just won't listen to what the rhythm of life's lessons is telling us. If we would only listen to the lessons of life, we would see that nobody can come into our lives and make us happy, special, or complete. We hold the keys to our own love. After all, the number 1 represents a whole.

THINGS TO THINK ABOUT

1. Are you pressured by the traditional opinions of what being single should be? Have you created a healthy definition of the single life for yourself?

2. Have you discovered the peace of spending quiet time alone?

3. Are you focusing your time and energy on self-completion and self-fulfillment? Or are you spending most of your time searching for a mate?

4. Do you feel pressured by family and friends to get married and have children because that's what they want for you? How do you feel about it?

5. Have you looked into the mirror and said "I love you" lately?

Real Life Is No Romance Novel

"This is it. This time it's really over . . . Are you listening, William?" Angela asked.

"Yes, I'm listening. You're breaking up with Dwight for about the fifth time in three years."

"This time I mean it," she blurted, her voice raised in a cautious anger. "He's been messing around with his ex-girlfriend. Somehow she has my unlisted phone number and she's been calling here harassing me. She said she was going to steal Dwight. She even claims she's pregnant with his baby." Angela sighed. "None of this would've happened if Dwight had been faithful and kept his pants up. It's bad enough having to deal with his baby's mother. She's always trying to get him back. I think he messes around with her too. I won't be disrespected like this. I've been good to him. I cook his favorite meals. Last week I helped him get his car fixed. I even let him get his phone turned on in my name. I've had it!"

"I don't want to say I told you so. But this is the same old story. You'll leave him and be back with him in a week as though nothing ever happened. Your life is a romance novel. Why don't you get a man with less drama and confusion? What happened to that nice guy who worked for the airline?"

The telephone beeped, signaling she had another call and interrupting her answer to my question. When she came back on the line with me, her tone had changed. She sounded better. The smile on her face was so big that I could hear it over the phone. "William, I've got to go. Dwight's on the other line and he wants to explain."

I've known Angela for three years, and she's been chasing Dwight the whole time as if he were the only man on earth. He's been dogging her and fooling around on her since the beginning. In turn, she's been issuing him ultimatums and leaving him when he doesn't respond. She has a regular pattern. After only a few days, Angela breaks down. To fool herself into thinking things are better, she rationalizes an explanation for Dwight's unacceptable behavior. She spends long hours at home or work staring out the window analyzing his every word or action until she can find something, anything, to make his lies acceptable. That way she can forgive him, salvage her pride, and save her relationship all in one fell swoop.

Her rationalization is a nice neat lie to fool herself. But what she has really done is tossed herself in deeper for the next chapter in her romance-novel reality. Dwight will never act right. He doesn't have to. He isn't lying to himself like Angela. He knows he can come in and go out of her life as long as he pleases. He can be with his baby's mother, his ex-girlfriend, or any other woman he chooses. In fact, he probably has similar dramas going on with them as well. He knows that it will only take some smooth words and a little pillow talk to straighten Angela out. It's worked for three years.

On the outside, romance is a lush, mellow, and juicy fruit. It's flawlessly smooth and firm to the touch. Take a deep bite. It yields a fine nectar, sweet on the tongue. A juice that sugar-glazes the lips and tickles the soul. But in the middle is the seed from which it all grew, the bittersweet core—as tart as lemon and as sweet as honey. It's the romantic tension. The pulsating energy that drives lovers together and pulls them apart. No romance is complete without it. It's a natural and essential ingredient for love. It provides a give-and-take. A yin and yang. This tension is nature's way of making love hot, passionate, and spicy enough to motivate us. Without it, love would be boring and never hold our attention long enough to grow into much at all.

Honestly, we all like some romantic tension in our lives. It starts with those early moments. The early feelings of wondering that one hopes will end in the arms of that special person. Will they ever call? Will you see them again? Awkward times of wondering when to hold hands, whether to hug, and when to kiss. Later in the story of romance, couples continue to feel it. Does he still love me? Do I still excite her? All of this romantic tension is as natural as the air we breathe.

Good examples of the power and importance of romantic tension can be found in romance novels. Boy meets girl in Hollywood. Boy meets girl in World War II. Poor boy meets rich girl. The scenarios change but the plots are consistent. Take a man and a woman, add a dynamic background, push them together, pull them apart with conflict, and an exciting romance will grow.

It may sound simplistic, but there is a lot of truth between the covers of a romance novel. Consider your own romantic life. Think about the lives of your friends. Surely you know of some stories that could be best-sellers. The pattern is there. Boy meets girl. Boy and girl fall in love. But then . . . Whether you've been with the same person twenty years or you're on your first date, the passion and anticipation are still there.

The most intense romances grow from conflict. What if Rhett had given a damn in *Gone With the Wind*? What if he had been a nice guy who catered to Scarlett's every whim? It wouldn't have been much of a story. It certainly wouldn't have been a classic. *Romeo and Juliet* would be a drab story without the tension between the rivaling Capulet and Montague families that ultimately brings the young lovers to their tragic end.

Healthy conflict is a normal part of a growing relationship. But what about Angela? Three years of ups and downs have not moved her relationship with Dwight forward one inch. She's caught in the cycle of a relationship that is not growing. Conflict in her relationship leads around in a loop to more conflict. Dwight continues to womanize at will, and Angela stores her true anger and pain inside. Either she can't differentiate conflict from romance or she doesn't want to. She seems attached to the confusion and drama her relationship with Dwight creates.

She never had the opportunity to answer my question about the nice guy from the airline. She met him around the time she met Dwight. But in a quick decision, Dwight won the race for her affections. The two men were very different. The few times she mentioned the guy from the airline, she remarked about the nice dates they'd had. She talked about how he opened car doors and called frequently—even when he was out of town. In spite of that, Dwight was stealing the show. He didn't open car doors, he broke dates, rarely called, and was living with someone when they met. He was the bad boy, the one who wasn't right. Angela wanted to change him. She saw him as a challenge.

Was Dwight's bad-boy attitude the attraction? Was it the challenge he posed? Is Angela prone to self-destruction? Some people listen to their hearts when looking for a mate. Some people choose mates according to a rigid list of conditions. Others, like Angela, seem to say they want one thing, but choose the opposite situations that are doomed from the start. She said she wanted Mr. Right, but chose Mr. Wrong. Good women do it every day. "Everything was perfect, but he was married.'' ''Everything was perfect, but he was living with another woman.'' ''Everything was perfect, but he was too in love with his career.'' ''Everything was perfect, but he was already dating my best friend.'' ''Everything was perfect, but he had a drug problem.'' ''Everything was perfect, but I couldn't share him with another man.'' ''Everything was perfect, but another woman broke his heart and left him hard.'' What good can come from a situation that is already doomed from the beginning?

Often what we know is bad for us is irresistibly tempting. The give-and-take of a romance offers both euphoric bliss and bitter anger. We all enjoy some of that romance-novel drama. Angela knows Dwight isn't a good man for her but she chases him anyway. But the trials of romance are for growth. If a romance is caught in an endless cycle of ups and downs with no progress being made, the fruit isn't ripe—don't eat it. If the relationship is growing from successful conflict resolution, the fruit is good. But if the whole thing is one giant never-ending conflict, the fruit is rotten.

Reality can be a tough pill to swallow. Letting go is hard, but it's better to be alone and free than a slave to lies and deceit. Unfortunately, I don't think Angela will choose to liberate herself. I envision her relationship with Dwight as a romance novel that will continue all of their lives. Dwight will come and go as he pleases, and Angela will always rationalize a nice neat lie for herself and take him back.

It reminds me of another friend whose romance-novel affair has been going on for over twenty years. She's an attractive businesswoman in her early forties who confided in me that she had been involved in a roller-coaster romance with the same man since her freshman year in college. Since that time, he married and had kids. To spite him, she married and had a child. He divorced. She divorced. He remarried and divorced again. She remained single. During all this time, they continued to see each other. They still see each other today though both are involved with other people. She says that her life has revolved around her old college love to such an extent that she's never really fallen in love with another man. She has spent the best years of her life going in circles with him. Angela is headed down the same road.

Is that true love? Not at all. Love isn't an easy ride. But it isn't self-destructive either. Angela's story is a romance novel with real characters. It's the continuing reality of lies and broken promises that won't end neatly on a page. Angela is making mistakes that will probably come back to haunt her. She has willingly closed her eyes to the truth and put her faith in a man who has proven himself unworthy of her trust and respect. One day Dwight is really going to put Angela's excuse-making for him to the test. One day something that she can't whisk away will happen, and all the years of excuses are going to blow up in her face. I believe that deep down inside, she knows that. She just doesn't want to admit it. For Angela, living the lie is comfortable. Unlike the truth, it doesn't require her to make tough life-changing decisions. But lies offer us no peace or security, only the illusion of them. I hope all the trouble Angela is going through with Dwight will help her to accept that fact before she has to learn things the hard way. But perhaps she won't see it until something undeniable happens. Maybe her life will have to come crashing down before she opens her eyes to the truth.

THINGS TO THINK ABOUT

1. Have you ever wanted to be in love so badly that you ignored what your better judgment was telling you about someone?

2. Does the idea of drama in a relationship excite you?

3. Do you make excuses for the poor behavior of your significant other?

4. Do you and your significant other work equally at constructive conflict resolution?

Fine Wine and Younger Men

Darlene and Kevin rushed up the steps to the glass doors of the church. For Darlene this was an important Sunday morning. She wanted everybody to meet the man she was so crazy about. They took a moment to straighten themselves out and catch their breath. Then they approached an usher—none other than Mrs. Nerline Bates. She had been serving the church by standing at the door of the sanctuary for twenty-five years. She had also been serving as the switchboard of the church gossip network for just as long. She looked Kevin up and down. Her eyes widened. Then she looked at Darlene, puckered her lips, and her eyes grew even bigger.

With Mrs. Bates as the megaphone, everybody in the sanctuary would soon know that the wonderful man Darlene had been bragging about for weeks didn't look a day over thirty. If he was even that old. This meant that Kevin was ten years younger than Darlene. Only five years older than her eldest son. And worst of all, roughly the same age as the daughter Mrs. Bates had been trying to marry off.

But why was this such a big deal? It may raise a few eyebrows when a man is with a woman half his age, but this doesn't carry nearly the taboo associated with older women and younger men. In fact, a man gets a pat on the back for wooing a younger woman into his life. It's a badge of honor that tells everybody the old boy has still got it. But a woman has to deal with friends and family telling her that she's too old for a younger man. That she's not acting her age. Jokes are made about robbing the cradle. People even imply that she's possessed by uncontrollable lust.

But despite those old taboos hanging around, there are more and more women reaching back five, ten, and even twenty years for a man. As things change in our society, we're finally turning away from the idea that a woman's life is downhill after she hits thirty, notices a wrinkle, or goes through menopause. Instead we're acknowledging that she's evolving into a more complete woman with each year. This is not a fad. Women taking younger men as boyfriends and husbands is a new way of life. Despite the old prejudice surrounding it, the hows and whys of this development make complete sense.

From the time they are little boys, men are fascinated by older women. Or should I say evolved women? Every boy has had a crush on an evolved woman at some point in his life—a teacher, a friend's mother, or a teenage babysitter. In the eyes of an eight-year-old boy, even a teenage girl is a worldly woman. I had my share of such crushes from grade school through college. It all stems from the fantasy that evolved women possess a special secret of life that can transform us from boys to men. And it isn't about Oedipus. For boys and young men, it has more to do with runaway hormones and curiosity than with anything else.

I remember having a crush in college on a young, attractive professor whose lectures put me in awe. Everything she did seemed so confidently sexy. Her gestures. Her authoritative yet feminine voice. Learning never looked so good or walked so well. I always found reasons to ask questions and stick around after class. Just talking to her was a thrill. In contrast, I couldn't really connect as well with most of the girls my age. Most of them were too busy talking about frat parties and nightclubs to hold my attention. They wouldn't have the wholeness my professor had for at least ten years. I liked what I saw in this evolved woman. She already had it all together.

That's what attracts men to women older than them. The prospect of a woman already being whole. To understand this better, we have to observe some social dynamics. Let's look inside the mind of a young, upwardly mobile man in his late twenties or early thirties. Typically he's ambitious, focused, and goal-oriented. He is either working hard to establish his career, struggling in his own business, or attempting to complete graduate, law, or medical school. With those dreams come the harsh realities. Years of sacrifice that will precede the realization of any tangible goals. Contrary to what some women think, most of these men do in fact want to get married and start a family. But they know that won't be happening any time soon. Quite frankly, at this point in his life what such a man needs is a nonstressful relationship with a low-maintenance woman or no relationship at all.

But by tradition, he's probably dating someone close to his age. Typically, many women in their late twenties and early thirties seem to be in a hurry to get married, buy a house, and start a family. This isn't a sinister plot by a woman to tie a man down. She's just seeking her dream, or what she thinks her dream should be. But the thought of all that extra responsibility is a nightmare for a man who is trying to get himself established. What happens is a collision of wills. The young, upwardly mobile man says, "Let's wait." He wants to put off marriage, a home, and kids until he is more established. On the other hand his young woman is saying, "Let's get married now and work together to build our dreams."

On the surface her proposal sounds fair. But most men have a tendency to be more methodical in their approach to planning the future. This is how we think: I'll graduate at twenty-one, finish law school at twenty-four, rise to partner in a firm by twenty-seven, start my own firm at thirty, run for judge at thirty-five, etc. Somehow between starting his own firm and running for judge, he plans for a wife and two kids to pop up on cue. Of course, that's going a bit too far with the planning. But that's how men think.

That's why it may seem that young, upwardly mobile men try to avoid relationships. They're afraid their dreams may be sacrificed. This, coupled with the tendency of men to be afraid of commitment anyway, makes these men look totally noncommittal. But this is actually a result of that clash of wills mentioned earlier. The young man sees his young female interest as being too demanding. Likewise, she has a bone to pick with him. She sees him as unwilling to make the sacrifices necessary for a commitment.

Enter the evolving woman. She has a car. She already has a home. She already has kids. Having more experience in relationships, she also has less delusions about love. She may be thirty-something, forty-something, or more. She may even have the body and energy of a woman half her age. She doesn't fit the term "older woman" because there's nothing old or outdated about her life. She's living to the fullest in the present. She hasn't put her mind, body, or spirit into a passive mode simply because of her age. In fact, she has aged beautifully into a fine wine. Best of all, she's not in a hurry for anything. And that's very appealing to a younger man.

But having said that, the truth about evolving women is actually something you have to read between the lines to understand. Note that I've used the term "evolving women" to describe women who are attractive to young, upwardly mobile men. I intentionally used this term because it indicates maturity but is not limited to a specific age. That's because it's not really the age that matters. It is a woman's overall wholeness that is attractive to young, ambitious men. Qualities such as a realistic outlook on life, patience, and self-confidence often come with the wisdom of years. But not exclusively. Any woman, of any age, with those qualities is an evolving woman.

For some people, this raises the question: "If an evolved woman is so together, wouldn't she prefer to be involved with an older, more established man?" Not necessarily. Actually, there are a number of reasons an evolving woman would see a younger man as an attractive mate. Evolving women often feel more comfortable with younger men because younger men aren't products of the old-school, male-domineering mentality. Men also wear out physically faster than women. Because of this, some women seek younger men for their youthful vigor, which more closely matches their own lifestyles. Also, on average, men die younger than women. That is another reason women seek younger men. Some are looking down the road to companionship in their golden years. Or a woman may have already tried the conventional marriage-and-kids scenario once or twice, in which she may have felt the same dream-robbing pressures that the younger man is trying to avoid. She can relate to his desire for a low-pressure relationship because she's looking for the same thing.

Once we throw aside the stereotypes, it seems that there are some valid reasons for evolving women and younger men to be attracted to each other. They can be a great pair. But it is important to note that all of this isn't true for everyone. This sort of relationship won't automatically be a hit. Being in a certain age bracket doesn't mean a woman is necessarily full of wisdom and willing to love with less pressure. There are plenty of young women out there who are already evolving into their own brand of fine wine. And there are plenty of women, middle-aged and beyond, who are still living in Cinderella land, waiting for Prince Charming and the glass slipper.

Furthermore, all younger men aren't mature enough to handle a relationship with an evolving woman. Some men, as the saying goes, act their shoe size and not their age. At this point in her life, an evolving woman isn't looking for her boyfriend or husband to be her son too. If her younger man is more concerned with the latest dances and frivolous socializing, and lacks maturity in matters of work and love, it's doubtful the relationship will work out. A successful relationship requires two mature adults.

The fact of the matter today is that when two evolved adults fall in love, they no longer have to be as age-conscious as in the past. Today we're seeing many old prejudices and stereotypes about age breaking down, because the number of failing relationships in this society is forcing us to consider alternatives to tradition. As we seek to match the more important qualities of relationships—such as honesty, fidelity, and integrity—we have to expand our field of available partners, because those qualities aren't limited to any particular age. A man in his late twenties or early thirties no longer has to see thirty-something or forty-ish women as out of range. Likewise, women who are thirty-something or fortyish or older have expanded their age range for eligible men to include younger men. "Age is just a number," the old adage says. Our attitudes about love and age are changing to reflect that attitude. This is because what we all really need most is not necessarily a traditional match in age, but a strong love that can endure the years.

THINGS TO THINK ABOUT

1. Why has it been traditional for women to seek older mates?

2. Have you ever been involved with a younger man/ older woman?

3. If you've never been involved with a younger man/ older woman, what concerns would you have about such a relationship?

4. Are women who are in love with younger men unfairly stereotyped in our society?

5. What is the age range of your ideal mate? Why?

Being Straight About Being Straight

There's lots of talk these days about who's straight, bisexual, gay, or lesbian. For heterosexuals, this topic used to be on the periphery of discussions on relationships. But now, because of AIDS (Acquired Immune Deficiency Syndrome), it's an important topic in itself. Don't skip over this chapter thinking it doesn't concern you, because it does. This discussion is important to everyone, married, single, male, and female.

REALITY IS STRANGER THAN FICTION

Those seeking or involved in relationships have always had many concerns to address: fidelity, honesty, money, sex, etc. Now one has to consider their mate's sexual preference as well. Are they being honest with you about their heterosexuality? Can they be happy in a monogamous heterosexual relationship? Today, these questions are relevant and need to be considered along with other issues to be addressed before entering a serious relationship.

If that sounds ludicrous, consider this. A married female friend once confided in me that she'd found a love letter written to her husband describing a very intimate encounter in detail. She was hurt and shocked. But she never confronted him. She fooled herself into thinking it was perhaps just left over from a one-night stand. Then a few months later she found another letter. It was in the same handwriting and it described another encounter. But something wasn't right with it. It didn't sound like the things a woman would say to a man.

She suspected it could be a man, but dismissed the thought. Soon afterward, she intercepted another letter to him, still in its envelope, addressed by someone named Steve. Same handwriting. Same details. Her husband was having an affair with another man.

A male friend once told me the story of his girlfriend's best friend flying in for a visit. He'd been with his girlfriend for almost a year and during that time she'd told him story after story about her travel adventures with her best friend, Lydia. Naturally he was excited about meeting Lydia. From all the stories and pictures, he felt he already knew her. The day after she arrived, he got off work early and went to his girlfriend's apartment because it was nearby. He had a key, so he just walked in. It was quiet. But he'd seen her car and knew she was home. Then he walked to the bedroom and opened the door. Lydia jumped and rolled to the side. His girlfriend pulled the sheets over her head and started screaming. Lydia was more than a "girlfriend."

Some people may be shocked by these stories. But it has to be recognized that these are realities in our society today. You can't tell if a man is gay or bisexual by looking at him. A family and kids doesn't mean that he's straight either. Same with women. Lesbian and bisexual women don't all fit the stereotypical butch look. Most of the gay and bisexual men and women I've known don't look any different from straight men and women.

Here's the problem. We live in a society full of fear, denial, and shame. Our society has always tended to move toward silencing those who are different from the majority rather than attempting to understand them. Evidence of that can be found in the existence of racism, sexism, ageism, and all sorts of other prejudices. One of these is prejudice against homosexuality. Our society's response to the idea of same-sex unions is homophobia. That psychological landscape serves as the backdrop of the fear that gays, lesbians, and bisexuals have about living their lifestyles openly. This is one big reason many men and women just won't tell you they have preferences for the same sex. They're afraid of the social backlash.

Instead some respond to the pressure of society by wearing a mask of heterosexuality. Many wear it painfully in fear that if their sexual preference were discovered they'd lose their jobs, friends, families, and, in some cases, their lives. It is homophobia that drives some gays, lesbians, and bisexuals to live underground. They talk of their painful masquerades of living straight in public and gay in private. Others, who have been bold, tell of their "coming-out" stories. The times when they held their breath and let their families and friends know who they really were. Some were excommunicated and some were embraced.

The heterosexual population needs to take note of this. Perhaps if people could openly be who they were there wouldn't be as many shocking revelations such as the ones mentioned at the beginning of this chapter. In those situations, everybody involved gets hurt. What would've happened if we had a society in which the bisexuality of the man and woman in those true stories was openly dealt with earlier in their lives? If we had a society in which people didn't have to live underground in fear? Perhaps they would've never even been in those heterosexual relationships to begin with. Or at the very least, they would've felt comfortable telling their mates the truth about their sexuality from the beginning.

The heterosexual majority has to ask itself if we are causing much of this masquerading as straight by our homophobia? By depriving gays, lesbians, and bisexuals of their individual human rights, we create many more problems. Even as a straight black male, I can understand the battles of gays, lesbians, and bisexuals. They experience prejudice just as I do. No matter who it is aimed at, prejudice is all the same, it's wrong.

"But I just don't understand how a brother could be gay with all these good single black women available," one woman said to me in rebuttal. But that's not the issue. A man's choice to be gay or bisexual has nothing to do with the number of available women. Nor is it because a man has never been properly "turned out" by a woman. Women who see an attractive gay man and think they could straighten him out if they had a night are fooling themselves. Homosexuality or bisexuality is based on something we really don't know the answer to. Some experts say it is a result of life's events, how a person grows up. Other experts say it is a question of biological predisposition. Who knows?

Likewise, men wonder why women would turn to each other for relationships. Too often when this topic of masquerading as straight comes up, it disintegrates into stories people tell about men who have been caught in the act. But of course there are lesbian and bisexual women in our society as well— some in secret, some out in the open. There are women both married and single who have female lovers. In my informal interviews and discussions, only a small number of the women said they were actual lesbians. Most of them who expressed interest in same-sex relationships claimed to be bisexual. Others said their experiences stemmed from curiosity or temporary experimentation.

As with men, the reasons women are lesbian or bisexual could be social or biological. But there is one interesting difference mentioned by some female bisexuals. Some of the bisexual women I've spoken to say they chose dual sexuality because men weren't satisfying their needs, particularly emotional needs. Therefore they are seeking out other women to fill that void.

But thinking any lover, male or female, could ever fill your emotional void is a fantasy. Women who believe this are incomplete, because they are searching for another person to make their lives whole. For such a woman, no man or woman is ever going to be the answer. She needs to love herself to become complete. Having a female lover won't guarantee a woman happiness. A woman can hurt a woman in the same ways a man can. She can cheat, lie, use, abuse, etc. The necessity of self-love is a human need, not one based on gender.

LET'S GET REAL ABOUT THIS
Hold the self-righteous criticisms. We can't judge other people. The bottom line is that none of us is God. I have my personal relationship with God and that's whom I work for and answer to. Other people have to find their path to God and report for work accordingly. What their instructions, missions, and paths are, I have no idea. I do know that it is a full-time job just managing my life. I don't have time to climb a tree and peer into anyone else's bedroom to see what they're doing.

The point here is not to make a judgment on people who have same-sex preferences. It is to point out that this is a real and serious issue today in heterosexual relationships. Everybody isn't being straight about being straight. There's a possibility that you have been in this situation before and didn't even know it. Some people will say: So what? What you don't know can't hurt you. But there's more to it than that. Obviously this question brings to mind serious health issues. It also raises questions concerning fidelity and honesty, the basis of any relationship. What you don't know can hurt you. This is not something you can afford to wonder about. It is something you have the right to know.

AIDS: THE DEADLY REALITY

This chapter brings up the uncomfortable subject of AIDS, something many heterosexuals would rather not discuss. But despite its being a topic many heterosexuals would rather avoid, we can't afford to ignore it. AIDS is no longer a virus that is associated only with homosexuals and intravenous drug users. Today, AIDS is attacking the heterosexual community at an alarming rate.

But despite the continuing explosion of AIDS, many people, especially heterosexuals, continue to conduct their sex lives as though this plague isn't happening all around us. Many of us continue to have multiple sex partners and don't practice safe sex. Many young, healthy, sexy people just don't think it could happen to them. But they are at risk and must read the warning signs we're getting on AIDS. AIDS is a real threat to any sexually active person. Just consider the following chilling facts about this killer virus.

FACT: The June 1997 issue of *Essence* magazine reported that 75 percent of the women in the United States with AIDS are black and Latino women.

FACT: According to the Centers for Disease Control, as of June 1997 there have been over 612,078 reported cases of AIDS in the United States. That's more than the entire population of Washington, D.C., as counted in the 1990 U.S. Census!

FACT: The Centers for Disease Control estimate the number of HIV-positive* people in the United States to be 650,000 to 900,000. This figure includes those who have actually tested positive as well as those who have the HIV infection and don't even know it.

---

* HIV (Human Immunodeficiency Virus) attacks a person's immune system and leaves it vulnerable to AIDS. A positive HIV test doesn't mean a person has AIDS. However, a person infected by HIV is at a high risk of contracting AIDS.

For more information on HIV/AIDS, contact the Centers for Disease Control National AIDS Hotline: 1-800-342-2437, or on the World Wide Web at http://www.cdcnac.org

POINTS TO REMEMBER
- Everyone isn't straightforward about their sexual preference or sexual history.
- Both men and women can pretend to be straight.
- Bisexuals, gays, and lesbians don't have a certain look that identifies their sexual preference.
- You have the right to know if your significant other has a sexual preference or sexual history that may put your health at risk.
- The number of AIDS cases continues to rise dramatically, particularly among African American and Latino women.

For more discussion on sexually transmitted diseases, see the chapter "Sexy Legs and Herpes Too."

THINGS TO THINK ABOUT
1. Have you ever suspected someone you were involved with was secretly bisexual?
2. Do you discuss a person's sexual history and sexual preferences with them before becoming sexually involved?
3. AIDS is a disease that can hide in your body for years. For that reason, regular testing is necessary. Have you had an AIDS test lately?

Black Women: Living Legacies

Black women have been faced with many obstacles through history. Today, things are better. But there are still some obstacles specific to the black female experience in our society. Just as their fathers, sons, brothers, husbands, friends, and lovers do, black women experience alienation, rage, and discrimination. They too are burdened with the baggage of unhealed wounds from centuries of enslavement.

Some people, both white and black, contend that black Americans dwell too much on the slavery experience. They assert that blacks should forget about slavery and move forward in the present. But so many of the wounds of the present are rooted in that past. Without acknowledgment and closure from that experience, blacks will be at a loss to understand their present and future.

For black women, the slavery experience has left many open wounds. As a direct result of those times, black women must contend with the idea that they don't fit the traditional American standard of beauty. They face discrimination both as black Americans and as women. They face wicked sexual stereotypes of themselves. Last and most painful of all, the traumatic events from the slavery experience have caused a backlash that reaches forward into today and often puts black women at odds with black men.

LIKENESS TO WHITENESS

The 1995 Miss Universe pageant was an ironic example of opinions on black beauty. The first irony was the location of the pageant. Of all the places on the globe to hold a celebration of Western beauty ideals, an African country, Namibia, was the location. A land where the Western ideals of beauty are contrary to the natural appearance of almost everyone. The second irony began the moment Chelsi Smith was crowned Miss Universe. Blacks all over America let out screams of victory when they saw the first "black girl" in history win the crown. But Chelsi is biracial (half black and half white). I have no qualms with her mixed heritage or with Chelsi herself. She's a beautiful and talented woman by any standard. It's not her facial features or shade of skin that I'm questioning. My curiosity is centered on the world's definition of beauty. Does the crowning of a half-black woman hold any significance or is it just a coincidence?

Remember when Vanessa Williams won the Miss America title? Think about the physical features of top black beauty queens and you will find an obvious pattern. Many have a striking likeness to whiteness. The American beauty ideal is based on long flowing hair, subtle facial features, fair skin, and light-colored eyes—a look that most white women don't even have. Our society proclaims women who have that look or close imitations of it are beautiful. That's why the top black beauty queens tend to have sparkling eyes and subtle facial features. Again, this is not to criticize Vanessa, Chelsi, black beauty queens, biracial fair-skinned women, or women with white skin, blond hair, and blue eyes. But the truth is the truth. If they were dark women with thick lips, full hips, and large rounded backsides, the chances that they would have received those crowns would've been significantly slim. Some would say they wouldn't have had a chance at all.

ODD WOMAN OUT

On another front, black women face very real discrimination. They face it as a double minority—as women and as blacks. First, as women, they have to deal with the traditional institutionalized barriers to their success. Too often they have to deal with people who have the out-of-style thinking that women shouldn't be in positions of leadership, in the professions, or in business for themselves. Women in the military, police work, firefighting, labor-intensive jobs, and even the clergy have to face the old "this is a man's job" mentality. Add to that the pressures associated with being a woman in a world largely run by men and one can see that climbing a career ladder can be difficult for a woman of any color.

But in addition to dealing with sexism, black women often face racism. It may be subtle, such as the "What is she doing here?" stares (familiar to all black Americans). Or it may be in the form of overt racist remarks or actions. Regardless of whether it is subtle or overt, racism creates rage and frustration and can still end careers. It continues to be a real obstacle for many blacks in the workplace; black women are no exception. And when coupled with sexism, it can feel overwhelming.

FROM AUNT JEMIMA TO JEZEBEL

Black women face some ugly stereotypes of themselves. In times past, black women were stereotyped as either Aunt Jemima or Jezebel. Aunt Jemima was the sexless, tireless, complacent matriarch who posed no threat to the established social order of the antebellum South. In contrast was Jezebel. She was the dangerous, sexually insatiable temptress. Jezebel was capable of casting mysterious voodoo-type spells over innocent and unsuspecting men, causing them to submit to her immoral desires.

Today, Aunt Jemima survives mostly as an icon and brand name. But even she has had a makeover. However, the Jezebel myth hangs on. It rears its ugly head in subtle ways every day. It isn't something that's openly admitted. But many people—including blacks—hold to the old stereotypes about black women possessing some mysterious type of "black loving." On the surface, that may not seem such a bad association. Some may even consider it a compliment.

However, we must remember that lurking behind sayings such as "The darker the berry, the sweeter the juice" are destructive sexual stereotypes of black women. Such phrases were created to reduce black women to the level of sexual beasts. Making them less human meant they didn't have to be regarded as women. Sexual myths set the stage for the abuse, rape, and exploitation of black women throughout history. We have to be careful not to forget their true meaning.

THOSE _____ BLACK MEN

Let every woman fill in the blank for herself. Hopefully the words will be along the lines of "wonderful," "industrious," and "resilient." But I'm sure some other descriptors will be inserted as well.

Unfortunately, one of the biggest battles of black women is with black men. I use the term "battle" because it's a constant give-and-take with terrible casualties on both sides. And like most battles, it could be better settled through communication. There's lots of misunderstanding, finger pointing, and a general lack of meaningful communication on both sides. Half the time we're too busy throwing rocks at each other to create any solutions to our problems. Men accuse women of male bashing and women accuse us of female bashing. Unfortunately, we do it on television every day for others to laugh at and profit from.

But we're too quick to blame our conflicts on each other as black men and women when that's not always the case. Like all cultures, we have our share of problems, but we are not inherently problematic people. Moreover, every hurdle we face is not the fault of the other sex. Many times we're experiencing the problems of human beings in general. The issue of men being less communicative, cold, and afraid of commitment aren't just the concerns of black women. Men not paying child support, walking out on marriages, and hanging out with their friends all hours of the night aren't just the concerns of black women either. Those are realities that stretch across ethnic and class lines.

Also, one should consider the influence of personalities and backgrounds when assessing men. All black men aren't the same. We are a highly diverse group of individuals. Within our ranks we have everyone from Dennis Rodman to Johnnie Cochran. From Mike Tyson to Cornel West. From Prince (the artist formerly known as Prince) to Colin Powell. From Clarence Thomas to Martin Luther King. From Rodney King to Jesse Jackson. From Tupac Shakur to Malcolm X. Does anyone in their right mind think that such men would all think the same way about everything? With such a diverse group of men, it's imperative to look at each one as an individual with his own mind and actions rather than as someone with preset actions and motivations. Just because one black man or several black men act a certain way doesn't mean we're all that way.

Despite that, I know that some sisters may have used some harsh words to fill in the blank. I'm sure a woman somewhere immediately shouted "lazy." Black men are accused of lacking motivation and ambition. I'm sure a woman somewhere shouted "abusive." Black men are accused of being violent and abusive with their women. I'm sure a woman somewhere shouted "dogs." Black men are accused of being promiscuous. But those generalizations don't apply to all black men. However, there certainly are brothers who fit all three of the descriptors. But there are also Anglo, Asian, Arabic, Latin, and European men who fit the mold.

I don't claim to have all the answers or excuses for the charges brought specifically against black men by black women. I can only submit a few things worth thinking about. Again, we must start with the history of the slavery experience. If you emasculate a man, leaving him powerless to provide for and protect his family, will that affect him? If a man is living in a land where money and power create the basis of manhood and he has extreme difficulty acquiring those things and even more of a struggle to hold on to them, will this affect him? What's produced is a man who will either somehow rise above it all, give up, explode, or channel his manhood into sexual conquests. Not excuses, just realities behind the statistics.

Today, black men are playing catch-up in a high-stakes game of survival. I know better than to think that most black women don't know that. I dare not believe that hype. I honestly believe that most black women are aware of the circumstances surrounding the past and present of black manhood and don't participate in male bashing. I can say, from looking at my diverse circle of female friends, that I don't have any female friends who wholeheartedly believe the stereotypes. Admittedly, I've heard them get down on brothers sometimes, but they don't dwell on negatives.

Fortunately, most of my negative experiences with black women have come from watching them on television talk shows or on occasions when I meet such women in public. When that happens, I really try to look at those women with love in my heart, getting past their negativity and realizing they have issues to work through. I also know that negative views and opinions don't represent the attitudes of most black women. Most are too proud of themselves and too conscious of reality to be professional male bashers. I believe the vast majority of black women are well-adjusted, hardworking women who have managed to maintain sanity and blossom despite the forces acting upon them.

As with every other group in society, black women have their good and bad apples. But the good ones are really sweet fruit. They truly embody a renaissance in womanhood that can be emulated by all women. Those who have combined the experiences of their black heritage with a healthy balanced approach to the rest of the world. Women who manage to balance incredible social and psychological factors and navigate through them. These women aren't brainwashed by the media images and the negative talk and statistics about themselves. They create and control their own self-images. They know the obstacles and challenges will never stop. But they've developed a successful self-confidence in spite of those things.

That self-confidence is the counterpunch black women need to fight back against the negative things said about them. A self-confidence that is found in the historical legacy of black women. A legacy mapped out by God. Black women of today need to be rooted deeply in their past. This is the connection that will launch them forward in the face of anything they come up against. Every black woman today should draw upon the spirit of her past. She is in the hull of the slave ships. She's in the scorching cotton fields. She's part of an omnipresence with her ancestry.

When Dr. Mae Jemsion was catapulted into the stars on the Space Shuttle, she rode on the wings of Bessie Coleman, the first black American woman to be a licensed pilot.

When Anita Baker sings, she joins in harmony with Billie Holiday and Marian Anderson.

When our souls are rocked with the poetry of Maya Angelou and the words of Toni Morrison, we hear the ruminations of Zora Neale Hurston.

Women such as Lena Horne, Ruby Dee, and Cicely Tyson forged the way for other black women on stage, television, and film.

Black women should never hang their heads low in shame. They have the grace of Nefertiti and the beauty of Cleopatra. Their sisters were the great Candace Queens who ruled Ethiopia, one of the first advanced and intelligent civilizations known to the world. They have the blessings of the ancient African queens. From Queen Amina of Zaria comes fortitude. She was a woman whose brilliant military leadership forged a kingdom. From Queen Nzingha, Amazon Queen of Matamba, comes courage. Her military leadership and political savvy drove out Portuguese slave hunters.

They are mothers. The mothers of the human race as well as the progenitors of black men. Every black man who has ever done anything great or bold started his journey as a helpless babe at his mother's nipple. The first time he felt warmth was from a black woman. The first time he felt secure was from a black woman. The first time he knew love was from a black woman.

This rich and powerful legacy is there for any black woman to draw upon. It stands as a challenge for her as well. To know she is a beautiful person. To radiate that beauty from her interior. To fight discrimination by educating herself not only in academia but in an awareness of her own culture and history. To work with black men and not against them or exclusive of them. She has to know that her role is not that of tradition but that of innovation brought on by necessity.

Her challenge is to do more than one role and to do it well. She has to be a stern competitor in her profession, a gracious mother, a loving companion, and a warm friend. She has always had to be a superwoman and has always risen to the occasion. Today, she has become bolder, stronger, and more beautiful. If a black woman ever has a moment when she feels her self-esteem slipping because of some statistic she's heard or a negative report she's read, she needs to take a moment to reflect on things. By remembering who she is and where she came from, she can instantly gain power. It doesn't matter what anybody else says, she's a living legacy of greatness.

POINTS TO REMEMBER

- Black women have to define their own image of beauty.
- Black women have not only survived but succeeded in the face of racism and sexism.
- Don't allow negative sexual stereotypes of black women deprive you of healthy feelings about your sexuality.
- Black men aren't the enemy of black women. Healing of the wounds between black men and women will only come through communication, not condemnation.
- The legacy of black women is full of exemplary role models. Pick some and study them. You can draw upon their spirits to inspire you through your journey in life.

Domestic Violence: Don't Be a Victim

- Women who were attacked by men they knew were more likely to be injured in the attack than women who were attacked by a stranger.
- Twenty-six percent of rapes and sexual assaults were committed by husbands, ex-husbands, or boyfriends.
- Almost 30 percent of all female homicide victims were killed by husbands, ex-husbands, or boyfriends.

Source: Bureau of Justice Statistics, National Crime Victimization Survey, August 1995.

Those are chilling facts. But despite the attention being focused on domestic violence today, women still find themselves victimized by violent attacks by husbands, ex-husbands, and boyfriends. With the consequences of domestic violence so terrible, many people wonder why women remain in abusive relationships, or get involved with abusive men in the first place. But the answers aren't as simple as the questions.

WHY DOESN'T SHE JUST LEAVE HIM?

That question sounds like the logical solution for battered women. But the realities are not so simple. For battered women there are a number of economic and psychological factors they must deal with in order to escape an abusive relationship. The economic realities are prohibitive for some women.

They may want to leave, but don't have the financial resources to do so. If they're not working, or are in a household that depends on two incomes, they don't have the means to provide life's essential items: food, clothing, and shelter. That problem is magnified if they have children.

The psychological realities are that many women, regardless of ethnicity, education, or socioeconomic status, have had their self-esteem severely harmed by an abusive relationship. Women who have suffered damage to their self-esteem as the result of abuse feel they can't leave the relationships; they're dominated by feelings of isolation and powerlessness. They believe they can no longer make it on their own. They're trapped in their world of abuse.

Even more saddening are women who suffer from such low self-esteem caused by abuse that they feel they can't leave an abuser because they deserved the abuse. Those women rationalize the batterer's behavior. They say things to themselves such as "He wouldn't hit me if I didn't make him so angry." They blame themselves and think they can change him if they do something differently to make him happy. They believe the abuser when he says "It won't happen again." But it probably will, or the abuse is probably already an ongoing problem. Domestic violence happens in cycles that involve abusive episodes followed by remorse, cooling down, and a honeymoon-type period that lasts until the next violent outburst.

For more discussion on women who try to change men, see the chapter "You Can't Change Him."

But the biggest reason women don't leave abusive men is fear. Abusive men have traumatized the minds of battered women and created in them a mind-set of fear, shame, and even guilt, which is brought about by a combination of emotional, verbal, and physical abuse. Such women are afraid that they or their children will be harmed or even killed if they attempt to leave the abuser. And the fears of battered women are well founded; as stated at the beginning of this chapter, "almost 30 percent of all female homicide victims were killed by husbands, ex-husbands, or boyfriends."

WHY WOULD A WOMAN GET INVOLVED WITH AN ABUSIVE MAN?

Most women who are battered didn't know what kind of relationship they were getting into. Abusive men can be charming, charismatic, and romantic in the initial stages of a relationship. Most of them have a Dr. Jekyll and Mr. Hyde personality. They may show one face one minute and an entirely different side the next. Hints about their abusive behavior may be very subtle in the beginning, if apparent at all.

Later in the relationship, abusive men may begin to be verbally abusive, such as hurling insults. Or they may be emotionally abusive by playing dangerous mind games, such as constantly threatening to hurt or kill the woman. Over a period of months or years, the abuse may escalate from pushing and shoving to slaps, punches, kicks, and choking. The physical abuse can lead to death.

HOW CAN WOMEN AVOID ABUSIVE RELATIONSHIPS?

The best way to prevent abusive relationships is to avoid them. The only way to avoid abusive relationships is to watch for the warning signs that indicate a man may be a potential abuser. If you see strong indications of any of the warning signs listed in the next section, don't attempt to rationalize the man's behavior. Making excuses for his behavior could be a dangerous, even fatal mistake for you down the road. If you are seeing strong warning signs, get out of the relationship, even if you think you're in love.

WARNING SIGNS THAT A MAN MAY BE ABUSIVE

1. Excessive jealousy

Some women think jealousy is a sign that men care about them. All men are capable of getting a little jealous at times, but excessive jealousy may indicate that a man wants to control you. Men who exhibit this behavior may be jealous of not only other men you may know but also your female friends, family, co-workers, even pets.

2. Attempting to isolate a woman from friends, family, job

The abusive man will attempt to separate a woman from her family, friends, and co-workers. This allows him to gain control over her. A man who requires a woman to sacrifice her friends, family, and associates as a condition of the relationship, without good reason, may be a potential abuser. Likewise, women need to beware of men who encourage them to become economically dependent. A man who encourages a woman to quit her job and stay home may be attempting to gain a position of control.

3. Habitual violent outbursts

If a man is in the habit of venting his anger through violent outbursts, this should be a red flag. All people blow off steam from time to time in the form of an outburst, but men who can vent their anger *only* by yelling and screaming, punching holes in walls, breaking out car windows, screeching off in a car, or picking fights with other men are probably dangerous to be involved with in a relationship.

4. Abusive language

Abusers use verbal methods such as public embarrassment, insults, and threats. Abusive language is a form of emotional abuse. But it can also be a warning that physical attacks may be coming later. If a man has a tendency to insult you or minimize the importance of your opinions and feelings, it is another warning sign you should heed.

5. Playing mind games

Another form of emotional abuse is playing mind games. Some abusers exercise control over women by creating a situation in which the woman is under a constant state of threat. The abuser's mind game could involve a physical threat against her or it could be linked to a financial condition, such as threatening not to pay the mortgage or not to provide his part of the money essential for living expenses. A more extreme method of playing mind games occurs when the abuser threatens to hurt the woman's children or a pet or even threatens to kill himself.

6. Shoving, pushing, grabbing

If a man is in the habit of pushing, shoving, and grabbing, this is an obvious sign that he doesn't see anything wrong with physically handling a woman to vent his anger. The question becomes: where will it end? It's obvious that this is a big red flag.

ESCAPING FROM ABUSIVE RELATIONSHIPS

But what about women who are already in abusive relationships? How can they get out? There are legal remedies available to abused women. But they're far from perfect. Calling the police and filing protection orders are often the only tools available. But both of those legal remedies are reactive, after the violence has occurred.

Many women file a protection order against men who harass or threaten and have a history of violent behavior. The protection order is issued by a civil or criminal court to prevent acts of violence. The protection order can order the abuser out of the home and to stay away and have absolutely no contact (including telephone and mail) with the victim. It can be granted on a temporary or permanent basis. However, the permanent order is not actually permanent. It lasts for only about two years. Also, protection orders are not going to give the victim twenty-four-hour security. The protection order simply gives the courts a quick way to deal with the abuser if he returns. Therefore the victim should remain cautious even after the document is filed. The protection order doesn't prevent violence; it reacts to it.

Women who file protection orders should also be aware that this may cause some men to become even more angry. This is because a protection order in essence locks a man out of his own life. He can no longer visit his own home or see his children. However, if all else has failed, perhaps a protection order is the only answer. But one thing is clear. Women in violent relationships must get out.

DEVELOPING A SAFETY PLAN

Women in abusive relationships usually aren't in a position to just walk out. Getting out requires a plan of action. Experts in the field of domestic violence have constructed what they call a "safety plan." The safety plan is essentially a woman's strategy to escape from an abusive relationship. Such plans should be customized for a woman's specific needs. Therefore, women who are developing a strategy to escape an abuser should call the National Domestic Violence Hotline (the toll-free number is listed at the end of this chapter), or a local shelter for battered women, to obtain more information on developing a safety plan or planning an escape from an abuser. Here are the basic components of such plans:

BE AWARE OF WHERE YOUR ARGUMENTS TAKE PLACE
Think ahead and try to avoid arguments in areas where an abuser could find a weapon to use or a place to confine you inside the home.

WHAT IS YOUR ESCAPE ROUTE?
Are there places in your home from which you can escape when violence begins—doors, windows, stairways? Think of an escape route before the violence starts.

WHERE WILL YOU GO?

Have a friend, relative, or shelter ready to take you in when you leave. Keep the telephone number of a relative, a friend, and the National Domestic Violence Hotline with you in the event you must escape. Always have enough cash with you for a cab.

BACKUP ITEMS

Get a safe-deposit box or ask a friend or relative to keep important items such as bank account information, checkbooks, credit cards, important legal documents, your health insurance policy information, copies of car keys, etc. You should also have a friend or relative keep a few changes of clothing and medications you need. A shelter can also make suggestions on where to keep your backup items. This is important because if you leave home, you'll need access to all these things.

POINTS TO REMEMBER

- No woman deserves to be abused.
- You can't change an abusive man's behavior; he needs professional help.
- Domestic violence happens in cycles; don't be fooled by an abuser when he is apologetic or remorseful.
- Pushing, shoving, choking, punching, or slapping are never acceptable behaviors in a relationship. **Violent behavior is never an indication of love.**
- Emotional/verbal abuse **is** a form of domestic violence.
- A court protection order can provide you with legal protection, but it doesn't place you under armed guard.
- Domestic violence is a problem that affects all ethnic and socioeconomic groups in our society.
- Alcoholism and drug abuse are not the only causes of domestic violence.

FOR HELP, CALL THE
NATIONAL DOMESTIC VIOLENCE HOTLINE
1-800-799-SAFE
TTY for the hearing-impaired: 1-800-787-3224

What Can You Do to Help Prevent

Domestic Violence?

1. Call the police when you suspect domestic violence. Be an alert neighbor; pay attention to couples when they are fighting in public or in the apartment or house next door. Call the police before things get violent.

2. If you know a victim of domestic abuse, let her know you are there for her when she is ready and able to leave. Help her construct a "safety plan." (See the section of this chapter "Developing a Safety Plan.")

3. Support shelters for battered women with financial contributions or volunteer a few hours a week at a shelter.

4. Educate yourself and others about domestic violence. Invite a speaker to your book club, community group, church group, or sorority meeting.

How to Recover from a Broken Heart

NERVOUS NAOMI

Naomi's breakup with her boyfriend had left her nerves split and frazzled. The breakup had also taken fifteen pounds from her slim figure. To make matters worse, she couldn't concentrate at work and was now on the verge of losing her job. Naomi's ex-boyfriend, Kenneth, had left her for another woman whom he'd been seeing the entire year he'd known Naomi. Suddenly he chose to move in with the other woman and dropped the bomb on Naomi late one night over the phone. Naomi's past three months had been a daze of tears, sleepless nights, and desperate unreturned calls to Kenneth seeking a reconciliation. Was it worth all that?

PROUD PAULA

"He was intimidated by me." That was Paula's rationale as to why her third boyfriend in a year had left her life. She convinced herself that all black men were intimidated by strong, independent professional women like herself. Still, behind all the pride Paula had some doubts. She kept trying to be loved but nothing was working out. In all her pride even she had to wonder: What am I doing wrong?

BITTER BRUCE

"From now on, I'm going to be a dog," Bruce said. He'd played Prince Charming to the wrong woman for the last time. He just found out that his girlfriend wasn't really working all those long overtime hours—at least not at work. She had a man on the side. After all the roses, candy, and expensive dinners Bruce had lavished on Lana, he was crushed by the news. He was even planning to propose and had already picked out a ring. But now after opening up his heart and being double-crossed, Bruce decided women didn't want to be treated well. He felt that he'd have more success if he "dogged" them. But this experience begs the question. Does a relationship with the wrong woman mean all women are bad?

———

It's highly probable that we will all have more heartbreaks before we meet the right person. When this happens, you have to work through it to get back into good emotional health. Avoiding damage to yourself is the important thing. Sort things out. Back away from life for a moment. If it is true that there are no accidents in the universe, that seemingly horrible experience had a purpose. Don't let the anger and tears throw you permanently off track. If that happens you'll miss the lesson that was in it for you and you won't grow. Instead of letting it defeat you, regroup and make your life better. Here are ten steps that will help you get back on track.

1. PUT YOURSELF FIRST
Know that you're important and worthy of love. Redirect your time and energy and focus it inward. Pamper yourself. Here's a list of things both men and women can do to pamper themselves: (1) Buy yourself something that you've wanted for some time. (2) Get your hair styled. (3) Get a massage. (4) Join a health club and get a personal trainer to work with you on an exercise routine. (5) Read some good books. (6) Take yourself

to breakfast, lunch, or dinner. (7) Put in your favorite tape or CD and go for a long drive. (8) Take a walk through the park or your favorite area. (9) Try a new activity or take some classes in school. (10) Pray and meditate.

2. ALLOW YOURSELF TO BE SAD AND ANGRY
Don't throw a pity party. But don't fool yourself and say that what happened didn't matter and that you don't care. Give yourself a few weeks to work through the initial sadness and anger. Being angry doesn't mean slashing somebody's convertible top or calling their place of employment and saying nasty things. It sure doesn't mean hurting yourself either. But screaming into a pillow, crying, or having a good venting session with a friend can go a long way.

3. DON'T COMPROMISE YOUR FEELINGS, MORALS, OR ETHICS JUST TO HOLD THINGS TOGETHER
No relationship is worth a compromise of your feelings, morals, or ethics. Regardless of whom you're involved with, your first responsibility is to yourself. If someone wants you to do things that you know aren't right, things destructive to your health and well-being, you don't need to be involved with them.

4. DON'T FOOL YOURSELF ABOUT THE TRUTH
Don't simply say, "He was intimidated by me," "She was too immature," or "He was just a no good dog," and simply chalk it all up to that. Demonizing the person who hurt you may help you temporarily by allowing you to vent some steam. But in the long run it doesn't have a redeeming healing value. Even if a person really did you wrong, you need to take a look at yourself too. How were you responsible for what went wrong?

What could you have done differently? Don't dwell on those things, but take stock and learn from your mistakes. Take responsibility for your actions.

5. ASSESS THE GOOD AND THE BAD AND LEARN FROM THEM

Despite a breakup being a bad experience, most relationships have had good times as well. While working through the bitterness of a breakup, assess the entire relationship. Just because you break up with someone doesn't mean you didn't gain anything positive from the time you spent with them. As for the negatives of the relationship, learn from them. Don't constantly get down on yourself about what you may have done wrong. Realize the mistakes you made and learn from them.

6. BURN THE OLD BAGGAGE

The scars from broken relationships are often painful and deep. Those scars can be so deep that we may inadvertently hold other men or women we meet accountable for the actions of the person who hurt us. Being cautious is a good idea because you don't want to fall into the same bad situation again. But it's not fair to hold the new people you meet accountable for the actions of someone else.

For more on this subject, see the chapter "Old Baggage Kills New Love."

7. KEEP YOUR OWN COUNSEL

It's not always a good idea to tell everybody about a breakup until you've sorted through what happened for yourself. You need to come to grips with things before everyone else starts adding their two cents. Some people will send you further off into pain with their reckless advice. Others will delight in your fall and turn it into gossip. Right after you break up you're at a delicate stage and could be unduly swayed by the opinions of others before you've thought things through yourself. At first, disclose information about your breakup only to a close circle of friends or family.

8. TALK IT OUT WITH THE RIGHT PERSONS

Instead of going public, talk to close friends, your family, your pastor, or a therapist. This step may come easier for women than for men. Accepting that we need help in handling a problem is probably one of the most difficult things for men to do. But a breakup can be extremely draining on the mind, body, and soul. Nobody is exempt from the pain and grieving that comes with breaking up, not even "macho man." Although some men may want to pretend breakups don't affect them, they are affected. But denial merely allows a problem to eat away inside you. Get it out of your system. Sometimes a friend, relative, or pastor is the best counsel, but sometimes someone who doesn't know you is better. It can be relieving to vent all your emotions and frustrations to someone you never have to see again. That's what a therapist is for.

For more on the subject of men seeking therapy, see the chapter "When You Can't Take It Anymore."

9. FORGIVE THE OTHER PERSON
FOR YOUR OWN SAKE

After a breakup, people are often consumed with anger and a desire for revenge. But if your thoughts and actions are motivated by anger or a desire for revenge, you're being controlled by the very person with whom you're angry. Until you let go of the anger and revenge, that person continues to claim a part of your energy. Let the anger go, forgive them for your own sake. Then your forgiveness of that person will free you to focus your thoughts and energy on yourself.

10. GO WITH THE FLOW

God has a plan. Not all relationships are meant to be permanent. Each one has a purpose and gives you new wisdom to help you along your spiritual path. Take the time to figure out what you learned from a breakup. Sometimes what you learned from a relationship is obvious. Sometimes what you learned may not be clear until much later. But we have to accept breakups as part of a bigger plan for our spiritual growth.

———

There's no magical elixir that can heal all wounds of love. Only you can ultimately heal your wounded heart. You're responsible for your happiness. Don't fool yourself into believing that another person has that power. Take the time necessary to learn to love yourself. Then two things will then happen. One, when you love yourself you'll find far fewer people whom you'll want to be romantically involved with because your vision of what you want in a relationship will be much keener. And two, those with whom you share your spirit won't have the power to easily control your feelings because you will go into your next relationship as a whole person, not as a person needing to be fulfilled.

I wish there was some way we could all prevent heartbreaks. However, despite the sometimes frightening possibility of heartbreak, there are many lessons of life and love to be learned from relationships. For that reason, it's likely that we may have many before we find a match for our souls. Going through the ups and downs of relationships has much to do with knowing how to spot the right relationship when it comes into your life.

Broken hearts can't be prevented, just made less severe. There's only one way to do that. Make sure that when that significant other person is gone from your life, you're there for yourself. Be confident in knowing that what looks to be a bad ending will always leave you in front of a new door of spiritual opportunity. We grow from everything that happens in our lives. And just as breakups are a part of growth, so are new beginnings.

FOCUS ON YOU

(Three ideas to help you get focused
after a breakup)

After a breakup, it's not unusual to feel sad or lose confidence in oneself. But it's important to preserve and build your self-esteem. Try these exercises to get yourself back on track during the vulnerable "post-breakup" period.

- Draw a line down the center of a blank sheet of paper. At the top of the left side, write "Things I love about myself." At the top of the right side, write "Things I'd like to change about myself." Focus your list on inner qualities. But it's fine to include financial and physical items as well.

- Read over the list of things you'd like to change about yourself. Set realistic goals for changing each of those items. Write each of those goals on a separate page in a notebook. Under each goal write a step-by-

step plan of action to achieve that goal. Be specific
and include a time frame and cost (if applicable).
Most important, construct detailed steps as to how
you will achieve those goals.

- On Post-It notes in various colors, write down a
personal quality you would like to have, such as
confidence, peacefulness, or patience. Put these "self-
empowerment" messages in places around your
home—preferably places that are personal and private
to you, such as your bathroom mirror. However, you
can also put them in public places inside the house.
I've often placed "self-empowerment" notes on my
front door so they are the last thing I see as I walk
out of the house.

POINTS TO REMEMBER

- Don't feel that the breakup of a relationship is all your fault.
- You are worthy of love.
- Anger and sadness are normal parts of a breakup. But it's not healthy for you to stay angry or sad too long.
- A relationship should not compromise your feelings, morals, or ethics.
- Take responsibility for your actions after the breakup of a relationship.
- Remember that you had good times as well as the bad.
- Don't hold new people in your life responsible for what someone else did to you.
- Share your sorrow only with people you can trust.
- Let go of the pain and anger, forgive the person who hurt you so that you can get on with your life.
- Realize that God has a perfect plan working for your life.

Ten Myths About Romance (Every Woman Should Know)

For years I've heard some wild advice that women pass along to each other. Some of it I've picked up from conversations. The rest I've gathered when some of these myths were applied to me. There's a belief out there that a set of guidelines about men can be your ticket to Mr. Right. I want to dispel these myths right now. Men aren't dogs that can be trained to sit, lie, bark, and cough up an engagement ring when women clap their hands. If your approach is based on that belief, it's a prescription for failure. Even if it works and you get a man to respond favorably to you for a while by using tricks and manipulation, what happens when he wakes up to it all? And, believe me, he will. One thing is for sure: he'll be headed for the nearest exit. But still some women cling to old beliefs as though they are a religion, believing that they can get what they want through deceit and insincere behavior. I've put the really big whoppers in the following list.

There are many, many false beliefs women have about men.

1. A real man will always make the first move
This is absolutely crazy. You can smile from across the room all night and he still may never speak to you. If you see something

you like, go for it. You don't have to rip your bra off and throw it at him. But a smile and a "hello" can go a long way.

2. If a man really likes you, he will go to any length to be with you

It is true that a man will make great sacrifices to be with the object of his affections. But believing that he should be willing to walk on hot coals or swim across the ocean to be awarded some of your time is totally ludicrous. If you're too inaccessible, a self-respecting man isn't going to keep calling for dates. He'll just brand you a game player. Or see your lack of accessibility as a sign of no interest in him.

3. He should always spend lots of money on you

All people spend money on what's important to them. But this myth is unrealistic for three reasons. One, it's economically impossible for a working man to wine and dine nonstop. Two, it will make a man feel like he's just being used for whatever money he has. He has feelings and wants to be appreciated too. Three, some men wrongly assume that they're entitled to sex when they pay for dates. For more on this, see the chapter "Who Should Pay?"

4. A woman should play hard to get

The strategy here is that a woman can gain control over a man she is dating if she doesn't let him know how much she likes him. The incorrect assumption is that the less she appears to be interested, the harder the man will work to gain her affections. But what this really does is make the man think a woman is playing games or just putting on an act. In either case, a man with the ability to see through it all will be turned off.

5. Men fall in love through sex

Nonsense. Men don't fall in love through sex. In fact, nobody does. People fall in lust through sex. Any woman who thinks she is going to keep a man in her life by keeping him in the bedroom is fooling herself. If there's nothing behind the sex, it can all get old pretty fast.

6. He must adore your family and friends and they must adore him

This isn't even logical. While we want all of our family and friends to adore our date or mate, and vice versa, it doesn't always happen that way. If they don't all click, that doesn't mean the relationship can't go on. Your friends and family can go on being your friends and family. Your husband or boyfriend can keep his role in your life too. The man in your life and your close friends and family don't have to adore each other, but they should get along amicably. However, a woman should take note if close friends or family have good reasons for not liking the new guy in her life; there may be trouble down the road that the woman is unable to see.

7. The man has to do all the driving

Here's a scenario. A man lives around the corner from a restaurant you both want to dine at and you live half an hour away. Why should he drive out to pick you up? If you have transportation it's far more practical to meet him there. The assumption that the man always has to be behind the wheel is sexist. The man doesn't always have to do the driving. Whether he wants to do all the driving is another issue. He just shouldn't have to do it just because he's a man.

8. Men don't know when they're in love

This is the assumption that men don't know what's best for them when it comes to love. Much of this is discussed in the chapters "You Can't Change Him" and "Real Life Is No Romance Novel." Lots of women believe this one. I've heard them make all sorts of excuses and rationalizations for men who aren't responding to their love. I've even seen them try to lead disinterested men to the altar. But I daresay these men actually do know when they're in love. If they aren't acting as though they're in love, they aren't. Usually women who say this are trying to make themselves feel better. Which brings up the question: Why would you even want to be in love with a man who can't figure out if he's in love?

9. The men who have the most money are
the best men

Money and possessions don't make a man Mr. Right. What does money have to do with his personality and spirit? If his six- or seven-figure income comes with 365 days of living hell, would it make sense to date or marry him? Also, most men don't make that kind of money. Sitting around and waiting for a prince or a sugar daddy is a mistake. Especially when you find out he's only human, no more or less than the men you may already know.

10. Married men make better boyfriends

This is not a joke. Some women believe the best men to date are married men. Why? I've heard answers such as "You know where they go home at night," "They don't mind giving away money and gifts," and, the most ridiculous of all, "They're more committed."

But, in fact, a married man who is cheating may not go straight home after he leaves his mistress. He may have several other women he's involved with. As for married men being more generous with money and gifts, they just see spending as the price of having "fun" with no strings attached. And this idea of married men being more committed is comical. If he's married, he's already committed. When he's with his mistress, he's being unfaithful. How can she see that as him being a more committed man? This has got to be the most ridiculous myth of all. Why would a woman wanting a commitment date a man who has pledged himself to a life commitment that he has already broken?

———

It's hard to keep a straight face through that list. I don't like myths, but I do understand the idea behind them. They're attempts to make understanding men, dating, and relationships simple, like a book of rules. Women who follow old myths and rules often feel they can avoid the pitfalls of love and relationships. But trying to approach men and relationships with a list of rules usually backfires on them, because they're getting old recycled advice about men from women.

Instead of playing games and looking for easy answers to the difficult questions of dating and mating, seek the answers from the source. Do something totally revolutionary and daring: Ask a black man to tell you about himself!

I have three suggestions for women who are trying to understand black men better:

1. READ BOOKS WRITTEN BY BLACK MEN ABOUT BLACK MEN

Tune in to what today's black men are saying about themselves. Read books such as *Speak My Name* (Beacon Press), an anthology of black male writers edited by Don Belton; *The Assassination of the Black Male Image* (Middle Passage Press) by Dr. Earl O. Hutchinson; *Black Men: Obsolete, Single, Dangerous?* (Third World Press) by Haki Madhubuti; *Makes Me Wanna Holler* (Random House) by Nathan McCall; and the classic novel *Invisible Man* by Ralph Ellison. But don't let it stop there. There are many other important black male voices in print. Reading them promises to give you a new perspective on the black men you may think you already know.

2. INTERVIEW A BLACK MAN

Sit down and objectively talk to a friend or family member. Choose someone with an even temperament whose opinion you respect. Sometimes a person you're not personally involved with will be more candid. Talk frankly about lust and love with him. Ask him the following questions and you may get to hear it all, the good and the bad.

INTERVIEW WITH A BLACK MAN ABOUT RELATIONSHIPS

1. Do you want to be in a relationship at this time? Why or why not?
2. Are you playing the field? If so, why?
3. Do you see a long-term relationship or marriage as the ending of fun and freedom in your life? If so, what could make you change that opinion?
4. Do you feel the women you've been involved with have

been more interested in you for what you could do for them or for who you are as a person? Are the financial and material expectations of women too high?

5. What special issues face black men in relationships?

6. Have you ever been hurt badly in a relationship? What happened?

7. What do you want women to know most about your feelings?

8. Have you ever been unfaithful during a relationship? If so, why? If you have been unfaithful, what did you learn? Would you do it again?

9. Can you be monogamous?

10. How important is sex to you in a relationship?

———

Another method is to have your book club, sorority, fraternity, church group, social club, or just a group of friends host a series of "Brothers, Lust, and Love" discussion evenings devoted to open communication between men and women. Mix a group of men and women with the hot discussion topics listed at the end of this book and watch the sparks fly. If everyone comes at it from the right angle, they'll walk out having learned something useful for their relationships with the opposite sex.

3. KEEP AN OPEN MIND

The most important suggestion I have for women who want to understand black men better is to keep an open mind. If you encounter one or several men in your life who fit stereotypes, don't fall victim to the one-size-fits-all mentality. Don't start stereotyping all black men and forgetting that each is his own person. The biggest danger in doing that is that one of the men you prejudge and look past may very well be a good potential mate.

THINGS TO THINK ABOUT

1. What myths about romance have you heard of?
2. Do you believe there's a set of rules that can be followed that will get you the man you want?
3. Have myths about romance had an effect on your love life?
4. Have you talked to men about the myths some women have about men to see if they are really true?

Brothers, Lust, and Love Hot Group Discussion Topics!

Here's a great way to have some fun and establish more communication and understanding between the sexes. Have a Brothers, Lust, and Love discussion night. Have your book club, sorority, fraternity, church group, or social group sponsor a series of discussions on the issues in this book. It's important to have as many men and women at the discussion as possible in order to assure a diversity of opinions. And invite me too. If I'm in your city, I may drop in.

I recommend using one of the following formats to make discussions entertaining, informative, and lively:

- A roundtable discussion with open rules, no censoring, a "tell it like it is" discussion.
- Panel of experts (be sure to include "everyday" men and women on the panel) and plenty of question-and-answer time.
- *Oprah* style. Have a moderator lead the topic and field questions.
- Try the "mixer" method. Have the moderator read an excerpt from a controversial chapter in the book, such as "The Ten Things Women Do that Drive Men Away." Then have each member of the audience anonymously write a question or comment on a sheet of paper and fold it. The moderator collects the

questions and comments, mixes them in a bowl, and randomly selects a question from the bowl. The moderator then reads the question or comment to the audience. If it is a question or comment about men, the moderator selects men in the audience to respond, giving women a chance to rebut the comments of the men. If the question or comment is about women, the moderator selects women to respond, giving men rebuttal time. It's important to have a time limit for discussion of each question.

Each topic listed has some suggestions for discussion. For more discussion ideas, you can refer to the "Things to Think About" and "Points to Remember" sections at the ends of chapters.

BROTHERS

• Issue 1: Do women expect too much from men in relationships?
Discussion points: Materialism in relationships, Sharing emotions and feelings in relationships, Sexual compatibility, Compromising vs. settling, Factors important to building a lasting relationship.

See the chapters "Mr. Right," "Are You Ready for a Good Man?," "Shoes Don't Make the Man."

• Issue 2: What's the right way to make a love connection today?
Discussion points: Singles clubs, Classified ads, Churches, Internet, Nightclubs, Activities (volunteer, political, etc.). Share stories and discuss the pros and cons of each.

See the chapters "Hello, How Are You?," "Say, Baby, What's Yo' Name?"

• **Issue 3: Why is being macho damaging to a man's life?**

Discussion points: Pressures on men, Male attitudes toward women, Men and their friendships with men, Men in therapy. Discuss how men can be more in touch with their emotions yet still be considered manly.

See the chapters "A Cure for the Tin Man," "When You Can't Take It Anymore."

• **Issue 4: Stereotypes of black men**

Discussion points: Media images of black men, Effect of damaging statistics on the image of black men, Are there conspiracies against black men?, Impact of stereotypes on black men in their relationships with women. Discuss the realities vs. the stereotypes of black men in America today.

See the chapters "What Is a Good Brother?," "I Am More Than Meets the Eye," and "I Need Your Respect."

• **Issue 5: Black male role models**

Discussion points: This topic requires some homework. Research African American and African men who are important in history and select several as examples of role models. Attempt to find a variety of men with a diversity of backgrounds and experiences, especially those who are somewhat obscure but did something honorable with their lives or careers. Try to focus on people other than well-known athletes and entertainers. Also, remember to consider the role models within your community, everyday working men, entrepreneurs, leaders, and professionals. Invite young African American boys to this discussion and introduce them to the role models. Start mentoring relationships with the boys and meet with them on a regular basis.

See the chapters "A Lesson in True Manhood," "The Good Daddies Club."

• **Issue 6: Dating when you have children**

Discussion points: Discuss how men and women with children can successfully balance the issues facing the child, their new significant other, and the parent who lives outside the home but desires to see his/her child.

See the chapters "Your Baby's Father or Me?," "The Good Daddies Club."

LUST

• **Issue 7: Let's talk about sex**

Discussion points: Casual sex, Monogamy, Extramarital affairs, Celibacy, What sexual practices do people enjoy today?, Homosexuality, Bisexuality, AIDS and sexually transmitted diseases, The spiritual aspect of sex.

See the chapters "Midnight Quickies," "I Thought You Were a Nice Girl!," "How to Have Great Sex," "Sexy Legs and Herpes Too," "I Want Your Soul," "Making Love from the Inside Out," "Being Straight About Being Straight."

• **Issue 8: Cheating: why do people do it?**

Discussion points: Discuss the excuses men and women use to cheat. Offer solutions as to how cheating can be avoided.

See the chapter "Her Cheating Heart."

• **Issue 9: Romance and finance: who should pay for dates?**

Discussion points: Discuss who should pay for dates and why. Be prepared to support your answer with strong reasons.

See the chapter "Who Should Pay?"

• **Issue 10: Light skin/dark skin: is it still an issue?**

Discussion points: Discuss ideas and prejudices within the black community about skin color. Can a black person prefer a particular shade of skin merely for aesthetic reasons?

See the chapter "Color-struck."

• **Issue 11: What does the word "friend" mean when referring to the opposite sex by married/committed people?**

Discussion points: Discuss how men and women can be friends without sexual overtones. Discuss what is necessary to make a spouse or significant other feel comfortable with your friends and associates of the opposite sex.

See the chapter "The 'F' Word."

LOVE

• **Issue 12: Interethnic relationships**

Discussion points: Stereotypes of black men involved with nonblack women, Stereotypes of black women involved with nonblack men, Mental and spiritual compatibility vs. skin color compatibility, Issues faced by interethnic couples, Raising children of mixed heritage.

See the chapter "Multicolored Love."

• **Issue 13: Women who need to know how to let go**

Discussion points: Relationships that drain your energy, Men who get you into trouble, Loving yourself first, Ways to let go of a bad relationship.

See the chapters "You Can't Change Him," "Real Life Is No Romance Novel."

• **Issue 14: Black female role models**

Discussion points: This topic requires some homework. Research African American and African women who are important in history and select several as examples of role models. Attempt to find a variety of women with a diversity of backgrounds and experiences, especially those who are somewhat obscure but did something honorable with their lives or careers. Try to focus on people other than well-known entertainers and athletes; kids already know who they are. Also, remember to consider the role models within your community, everyday working women, entrepreneurs, leaders, and professionals. Invite young African American girls to this discussion and introduce them to the role models. Start mentoring relationships with the girls and meet with them on a regular basis.

See the chapter "Black Women: Living Legacies."

• **Issue 15: May-December relationships**

Discussion points: Stereotypes about women being involved with men who are younger than they are, Mental and spiritual compatibility vs. age, Issues involving having biological children and adoption for women who are involved with men younger than they are.

See the chapter "Fine Wine and Younger Men."

• **Issue 16: Single and complete**

Discussion points: Family and social pressures on single people to get into a relationship or to marry, What are some stereotypes of people who are single?, Adopting or having biological children as a single person, How to be single and complete.

See the chapter "Single and Complete."

• **Issue 17: Domestic violence: don't be a victim**

Discussion points: Avoiding abusive relationships, Escaping from abusive relationships, Preventing abusive relationships.

See the chapter "Domestic Violence: Don't Be a Victim."

• **Issue 18: Why do men fear love?**

Discussion points: Men connecting with their feelings and emotions, Fears men have about losing their individualism in a relationship.

See the chapters "A Cure for the Tin Man," "Nothing to Fear."

• **Issue 19: What things do women do that irritate men?**

Discussion points: Using the chapter "The Ten Things Women Do That Drive Men Away" as an opening, discuss some of the most common complaints men have about their relationships with women. What are some common complaints women have about their relationships with men? How can men and women work together to address these issues?

• **Issue 20: Surviving a breakup and moving on**

Discussion points: Discuss ways to heal from the pain, guilt, and remorse that often comes with the breakup of a relationship.

See the chapters "How to Recover from a Broken Heart," "Old Baggage Kills New Love."

• **Issue 21: How good is the advice women give each other about men?**

Discussion points: Using the chapter "Ten Myths About Romance (Every Woman Should Know)" as an opening, discuss some of the most common myths women tell other women about men and romance. What are some myths men tell other men about women and romance? How can men and women work together to address these issues?

**VISIT THE BROTHERS, LUST, AND LOVE
INTERACTIVE WEBSITE**
http://www.williamjuly.com

- Send e-mail directly to the author, William July.
- Read William July's column, "Positive Energy."
- Keep posted on events and book-signing dates.
- Participate in discussions about the issues in *Brothers, Lust, and Love.*
- Speak your mind in public opinion polls.